Guys and Other Things
That Fry Your Brains

Guys and Other Things That Fry Your Brains

18 AWESOME SHORT READS

Nancy Rue

SERVANT PUBLICATIONS
ANN ARBOR, MICHIGAN

Vine Books is an imprint of Servant Publications especially designed to serve evangelical Christians.

Published by Servant Publications
P.O. Box 8617
Ann Arbor, Michigan 48107

Published in association with the literary agency of Alive Communications, Inc., 1465 Kelly Johnson Blvd., Suite 320, Colorado Springs, CO 80920.

Cover design: Left Coast Design, Inc., Portland, OR
Cover illustrations: Krieg Barrie

99 00 01 02 10 9 8 7 6 5 4 3 2 1

Printed in the United States of America
ISBN 1-56955-126-X

LIBRARY OF CONGRESS CATALOGING-IN-PUBLICATION DATA

Rue, Nancy N.
    Guys and other things that fry your brains : eighteen awesome short reads / Nancy Rue.
        p. cm.
    Summary: A collection of short stories conveying spiritual truths which relate to getting along with siblings, building trust with parents, guy-girl relationships, and handling life's setbacks.
    ISBN 1-56955-126-X (alk. paper)
    1. Conduct of life—Juvenile fiction. 2. Children's stories, American.
[1. Conduct of life—fiction. 2. Christian life—fiction. 3. Short stories.] I. Title.
PZ7.R88515Gv 1999
[Fic]—dc21   98-45163
                                                              CIP
                                                              AC

FOR

THE BEAUTIFUL FEET.

YOU KNOW WHO YOU ARE!

CONTENTS

Here it is—a dynamite collection of some of the best fiction you'll ever read. You'll laugh and cry with characters who are just like you—happy, confused, searching, *real*.

Nancy Rue makes fiction come to life like no one else. That's why we keep using her stories over and over and over again in *Brio* magazine. And since thousands of teens keep asking for more, we decided to give it to you—all bound together in one book—the best of the bestest from *Brio*. Enjoy!

Susie Shellenberger,
Editor, *Brio* magazine

INTRODUCTION

A short story collection. Isn't that something they try to make you read in English? You know—*The Collected Works of Nathaniel Hawthorne* or something. And, hey, isn't that where they make you read the story and answer the questions at the end?

Not this time. In fact, if anyone tries to make you write anything about these stories, let me know! We're not talking preach-at-you-till-you-drop-out-of-the-seat here. This gathering of stories is—well, maybe I can explain it best by telling you *why* I've put it together.

When I was a high school teacher—up until the year I decided to graduate with the Seniors—I noticed you girls get talked *at* a lot. There isn't anything "they" won't lecture you about. I mean, nothing is sacred. They'll tell you more than you ever wanted to know about everything from drug abuse to terminal acne. I recall one seminar on preparing for the *prom*, for Pete's sake!

But it was a rare thing to see a girl come out of one of those presentations jazzed about the life-changing experience she'd just had—unless—*unless*—the presenter had told the story of her own situation and how she dealt with it. Then the girls would talk about it almost longer than I could listen to them.

It occurred to me back then, as it does now, that it makes a whole lot of sense to just tell the story and let the listener relate it to her own life and draw her own conclusions. When you think about it, that's basically what the Bible is: a huge volume of people telling how it went down for them. Jesus himself was the ultimate storyteller—and even though the disciples sometimes whined because they were confused, they actually "got it" most when Jesus spun one of his tales. I figure I have almost that many stories in my personal collection—why not put them together for the same reason: so you can think about them and maybe even find a connection with your own experience.

The other thing that poked at me constantly when I was teaching high school, and still does as I live with my now-graduated daughter Marijean, is that girls in high school don't have enough time to read just for themselves. It seems like on the average day, a high school student hits the sidewalk running and doesn't stop until she drops into bed at night—probably with the last of her homework still in front of her—and chances are it's something incredibly fascinating like *The Collected Works of Nathaniel Hawthorne.*

If it isn't six and a half hours of tests, hall passes, and oral reports, it's a chain of club meetings, sports practices, and play rehearsals *after* school. Pile nine pounds of homework, parentally "suggested" chores, and a possible part-time job on top of that, and the idea of sitting down and reading a book just for grins falls somewhere in the you've-got-to-be-kidding-me category.

But I thought, what about a book you can pick up when you're climbing into the bathtub (you do make time to bathe, don't you?) or getting into bed (on those rare nights when you're finished with Nathaniel Hawthorne before your eyes slam shut)? What if it's not one big old long honkin' novel but a bunch of short pieces, each complete in itself, that you can read before you doze off or shrivel up? Better yet, how about if each were written about a real life conflict that you might possibly have faced?

That's actually how I try to write my stories. I spend a lot of time talking to teenage girls, and the only thing that gives me more pain than the fact that they have no time to just *be*, is that they have so much *stuff* hitting them in the face all the time. They've got to cope with obnoxious brothers, bossy sisters, controlling parents, pushy relatives. Some of their biggest problems are wrapped around the very people who are supposed to help them untangle the snags—their girlfriends. Then there are *guys*, and the inevitable baggage that comes with them—how to attract one and what to do with him when he gets into your life. And as if that weren't enough, there are the ever-present fears of the what's-ahead to deal with: Who am I? How do I make the right decisions? Am I ready for the future?

When girls talk to me about stuff like that, it doesn't occur to me to give them answers. I don't always know what would work for them right away anyway. When I do get a handle on it, it never fails, and I mean never—the answer is God. Before you either roll your eyes or give an automatic nod, let me say this: I am *not* a fan of bumper-sticker clichés like "Let go and let God" and "When God closes a door he opens a window." I mean, I know they're true, but it's way too easy for us adults to hand them out like business cards and expect you to know how to apply them. If I hear a sermon that does that, I have the urge to stand up on the pew and yell, "Tell me *how!*"

So when I see *how* God can work in a situation, I turn it into a story. When a group of girls told me they felt like they were becoming a self-protecting Christian clique, I found myself writing, "The Closed Club." A girl whose mom resented her friendship with another adult female found its way onto the page as "Move Over, Mom." A special young friend of mine who totally transformed herself for her boyfriend unwittingly helped me spin out "Always Blonde Enough." When God seems to say, "Come write with me," I do!

What you have in your hands, then, is a book you can keep under the mattress or in the basket beside the bathtub. You can delve into the lives of girls like you or your friends for ten or fifteen minutes at a time—and maybe come out with some ideas for looking at your own "stuff." What you'll find in every one is concrete evidence that a relationship with Christ works, even in a hit-the-sidewalk-running life like yours.

So while Nathaniel Hawthorne has his place (I still like his *Scarlet Letter* better than Demi Moore's)—this collection is written especially for you, the girl with a whole lot of things to think about and not much time to do it. My prayer is that you'll love the stories, maybe get some stuff you can use, and find out how close God is when you're thinking about guys—and other things that fry your brains.

Your Sister in Christ,
NANCY RUE

INSANITY BEGINS

AT HOME

MY BROTHER, MY FRIEND

MICHAEL: Hey, Blondie, I'm still hungry. Wanna go get a
           milkshake?
MANDY: You buying?
MICHAEL: Why? Don't you have money?
MANDY: Yeah.
MICHAEL: Really?
MANDY: Yeah.
MICHAEL: Can I have some?
MANDY: In your dreams!
MICHAEL: Get your shoes on and meet me in the Jeep.

I put that conversation in my journal, for the record.

Why, you ask?

Because it may be one of the most significant dialogues in history, right up there with the Lincoln-Douglas debates.

Because it took place between two people who just a few months before were still calling each other *Pizza Face* and *Miss Piggy* and preferring not to be seen in the same room, car, or restaurant booth by their respective friends.

Because that conversation took place between me—and my brother.

It was so weird. Ever since I can remember, Michael and I had been fighting—over who had the bigger piece of cake or who got to ride in the front seat on a three-block ride to the grocery store. We couldn't even sit down to watch TV without going to battle over what show to watch or who was going to hold the remote control.

"You two used to play so cute together when you were little," Mom said to us one day when Michael was snapping me with a towel during a dishwashing session.

"You've got us confused with somebody else's kids, Mom," Michael said.

"I wish you *were* somebody else's kid," I muttered.

"I think you *are* somebody else's kid," he muttered back.

That may not seem weird. This is what's weird. When I started high school, two years behind Michael, things gradually changed. It started when I brought home my class schedule the first day. He was in the kitchen, foraging, and I went in to catch any crumbs that might be left over.

"Who do you have for geometry?" he said.

Dazed, I looked around the kitchen. "Who—me?" I said.

"I don't see anybody else in here."

"Cranston," I said.

"No way! Get out of that class or you'll never see the light of day until after the final."

"But I can't get a schedule change now! They said—"

"Forget 'they.' There are ways. I'll get you out of there. Who've you got for English?"

"Getz."

"Cool. Biology?"

It wasn't until later that it hit me that we'd gotten through an entire conversation without snarling. I didn't even slam my door when I went to my room.

I thought at first it was just a mental lapse he had, that maybe he mistook me for some stranger passing through the kitchen. But that wasn't the end of it.

The next week he got his license, and naturally he looked for every excuse to drive the car. Mom caught on fast that he could now do taxi duty, and he started carting me to gymnastics and choir practice and Liz's house. He didn't complain—I mean, it got him behind the wheel.

During those rides, he started coaching me on how to get through Getz's essay tests and teaching me what the clutch was for. It was during those rides that we started calling each other Bro' and Blondie instead of Pizza Face and Miss Piggy.

Now, mind you, we weren't making a pact to name our firstborns after each other or anything, but I was definitely convinced that if my skin accidentally touched his he wasn't going to scream and run for the cootie-killing spray. It was obvious he thought I was OK. And then that one Friday night I was really convinced.

It was Michael's first weekend night to take the car out. He was supposed to be in by eleven. At 11:15 he called.

"Flat tire," I heard Dad say when he hung up the phone. "I tried that story when I was sixteen. Does he think we're stupid?"

"I think 'lame' is the word they use now," I heard Mom say.

It occurred to me right away that maybe Michael *had* had a flat tire. That didn't occur to our parents until he came home and showed them the spare on the right rear and the flat in the trunk.

"Oh. OK," Dad said. "It's late. Let's get to bed."

Michael was the first one to go—and he did slam his door.

I didn't blame him. When around midnight I heard him come out of his room, I followed him to the kitchen. Michael always grazed when he was upset.

"He could have at least apologized for not believing you," I said, handing him the peanut butter he couldn't locate because males can never move anything to find what they want.

"No doubt. It's like they raise this good Christian son—and then look for reasons not to trust me. Why is there never anything to eat in this house?"

"Because *you* live here," I said. "There's cold pizza in the meat drawer."

"How come you always know this stuff?"

"I'm female."

He looked at me for a minute, as if he'd never considered that fact before. Then he plopped a plate of Mom's homemade pizza on the snack bar and scraped a stool up to it.

"Want some, Blondie?" he said.

"Sure. I love acid indigestion."

"I'll split a bottle of Pepto-Bismol with you later."

From there on, it was, how do I describe it? A special night.

We talked about everything—how glad we were that Mom and Dad had raised us to be Christians and what had made us commit ourselves to Christ. We shared bummer stories about kids putting us down because we didn't swear and pressuring us to come to drinking parties. By the time we'd gotten the pizza down to the crusts, we'd even told each other how we prayed.

"You know what's cool?" he said.

"What?"

"We used to hate each other. Now we pray to the same God."

I was awake a long time that night. I couldn't go to sleep

until I finally put something together: If you share the most secret part of yourself with a friend, you get a little nagging doubt later because you're afraid they might tell somebody else. But when your friend is your brother, you don't have that, because you can trust him. He's family.

"'Night, Blondie," he said outside my door.

"'Night, Bro'," I said.

After that I started recording in my journal stuff we talked about in the car—just for the record—like jokes we told—even whole conversations. It was like I had this new friend.

And then that Tuesday afternoon happened.

About 3:30 I went into the kitchen to empty the dishwasher and found Michael in there with two of his basketball buddies, Jason and Scott. They were sitting at the snack bar practically salivating, and Michael was pulling open drawers and slamming cabinet doors.

"Do you have a search warrant?" I said.

"I smell brownies—I know Mom made brownies."

"Mom and Dad are gone until after dinner," I said. "She made us a casserole *and* brownies."

"Where are they?"

I lifted the lid of the cookie jar and pointed in.

"Thanks, Miss P," he said, and pinched my cheek.

Pinched my cheek. I stared at him as he tucked the cookie jar under his arm and plopped down at the snack bar with it. I should have known what was coming right then.

"We got any milk?" he said, his mouth crammed with brownie.

The hair started standing up on the back of my neck. "Try the refrigerator," I said.

"Hey, she's pretty good," Scott said.

Michael gave me a drop-dead look and said, "She thinks she's good."

I wasn't sure what was going on, and I'm sure my face showed it. I turned my back on him and started yanking glasses out of the dishwasher.

"You're a freshman?" someone said behind me.

I turned to find Jason chewing thoughtfully and watching me.

"Unfortunately," I said.

"I thought Michael was lying. You don't look like a freshman."

"Give her time, man. She'll catch up." Michael stared intently at the milk he was pouring. "She hasn't lost all her baby fat yet."

Before I could hurl a stack of plates at him, Jason said, "No—I mean, you look older than that. I saw you working out with the JV girls' basketball team the other day and I went, 'Whoa, what's that junior doing with all those freshmen?'"

Michael proceeded to choke on a brownie and lunge for his milk glass. I tried to kill him with one piercing glare, but he kept gasping for air.

"Really—you're pretty good," Jason said to me. "You oughta come shoot some baskets with us."

Michael made a miraculous recovery and yelled, "Not!"

"You afraid she'll make you look bad?" Scott said.

"Nah. I'm afraid we'll hurt her." Michael held out his empty glass to me. "Why don't you put this in the dishwasher before you run on along, huh?"

I didn't "run on along." In fact, I'm pretty proud of the exit

I made. I smiled sweetly at them all, except for Michael at whom I curled my upper lip, and then I swept from the kitchen with the cookie jar in hand.

What I really wanted to do was dump the whole thing over Michael's head and yell, "Eat them all, Pizza Face! I hope you turn into one big zit!"

By the time I got to my room—and slammed the door— every inch of me was stinging. I'd played Michael's game, and maybe even won, but the fact that he'd started it to begin with hurt me inside and out. I whipped out my journal and started scribbling.

"So much for our 'friendship,' Brother," I scrawled.

That was as far as I got. I wanted to go on with, "I hate him. I *hate* him. He made me look like a fool in front of his friends, when I thought I could trust him to treat me like a person. He made me think I could—and I can't—and I hate him!"

But I couldn't write it, because I didn't hate him. I loved him. In the last couple of weeks I'd really started to figure out who he was, and I liked what I was finding out. I wanted the relationship with him that he'd shown me we could have, and now he was playing around with it like it was one of his stupid basketballs.

I tossed my pen across the room. Maybe my parents were right. You could raise this good Christian son, but you really couldn't trust him to behave like one.

I pulled a brownie out of the cookie jar, but before I could stuff it in my mouth I stopped. And what about me? What about the sweet exit I'd just made from the kitchen? Was I any better? I mean, now what? Was I going to sit around and wait for him to make the next move? Or was I going to make like a

Christian and love instead of hate?

I hate to admit it, but just then I wasn't sure. I didn't find out myself until later.

Around 6:00 I heard Michael in the kitchen. He must have opened the refrigerator door five times without taking anything out.

My mind was saying "I hope you starve," but my feet took me out there, where I opened the door to the fridge, moved the milk carton, found the casserole, and popped it into the microwave. I felt like a robot, the way I was moving, and Michael wasn't much looser. He stood in the middle of the kitchen and mumbled, "Will we need ketchup for that?"

"I would assume so," I said, my voice chilly. "You put ketchup on just about everything, don't you?"

He made one attempt to locate the bottle and then barked, "Where the Sam Hill is it?"

That's when I knew what I was going to do.

I turned around and plastered myself against the pantry door. "It's in here," I said. "But you're not getting it until you answer a question for me, so unless you want to starve, you better be honest."

Michael rolled his eyes and plunked himself down at the snack bar.

"Why would you start a really good friendship with some-body—and then turn on them?" I said. "You know, make them look stupid in front of people, that kind of thing?"

Michael lifted his lip. "I wouldn't. I would never do that! Ask any of my friends."

With a leap I left the pantry and whirled to face my reflection in the oven door. "Mandy," I said to it, "you're one of

Michael's friends—or at least I thought you were. Has he ever done that to you?" I put both hands up to my face. "Why, yes, as a matter of fact, just today he made a total fool out of me in front of two guys. All this time he's been treating me like a real person, but he doesn't seem to want his friends to know that. After all—I'm his little sister—gross!"

"Oh come on, Mandy!" Michael said. "I was with my—it's a whole different gig—"

I spun around to face him. "I wasn't going to horn in on your whole afternoon. I'm not interested in going out and shooting baskets with you. And even if I were, did you really think I was going to stand there and whine because you guys wouldn't give me the ball?" I came at him at the snack bar and slapped my hands on the counter. "I just want to be treated with respect—because that's what I've learned to show you. And it has to be all the time—not just when nobody's looking."

The microwave dinged and I flung it open. "Stir it and put it in for three more minutes on high," I said as I headed for the door. "I'm not hungry anymore."

"Hey—" he said.

"The ketchup's in the pantry!"

"No—Mandy—wait!"

I stopped, but I didn't turn around.

"Look," he said behind me. "I know I was a jerk. I knew that I was doing it—and I'm sorry. It's just—I thought you'd think you were supposed to hang around with me all the time—"

I looked at him then, and I just shook my head. "It's kind of like a friend of mine once said. Why would you raise this cool sister, and then look for reasons not to trust that she would always be cool?"

When I got to my room I didn't slam the door, so it was still open when about an hour later Michael poked his head in.

"Hey, Blondie, I'm still hungry," he said. "Wanna go get a milkshake?"

"You buying?" I said.

"Why? Don't you have money?"

"Yeah."

"Really?"

"Yeah," I said.

He looked at me innocently. "Can I have some?"

I snorted and threw a pillow at him. "In your dreams!"

A grin broke over his face as he tossed it back. "Get your shoes on and meet me in the Jeep."

He gave me a look then—a look that said I'm sorry and I love you and I respect you and I'm glad you're my kid sister.

I couldn't record that in my journal. I just kept it in my heart.

TWO SISTERS

Once upon a time there were two sisters. They were so loving and kind to each other, that even the sun marveled at their affection and shone on them everyday—

"Oh brother," I said directly to my pen, just before I stuffed it viciously into my mouth and bit on it. "Hold onto your breakfast, kids."

"What?"

I glanced up at my sister Becky. Last time I'd looked at her she'd been leaning over the seat in front of us, organizing Rachel Kelly's life for her. Now she was gazing quizzically at me—ready, I was sure, to organize *my* life for me.

I shrugged. "Nothing," I said.

"I wish you'd quit muttering, Sara," she said. "If you've got something to say, just say it."

Actually, I had plenty to say. Like that I had a short story due in Creative Writing class in two days and I couldn't get past the opening line. Like that if I blew this, I knew I was never going to be the next Danielle Steele.

But spilling all of that to my older sister on the school bus was like coming right out and asking to be analyzed, advised, and completely rearranged right there on the spot.

The bus slowed down in front of the high school, and Becky was on her feet before it rolled to a halt, gathering up her letterman jacket and her drill team flags and her student council posters.

"See you after school, right?" she said.

"Uh, yeah, I was planning on riding the bus home like usual."

"You know what I mean, Sara," she said. Her voice was rising to big-sister-lecture pitch. "Not on the bus. At the drill team meeting."

I sighed.

"Now don't start," she said.

I hadn't planned on "starting." I knew she wouldn't give me a chance.

"I know you don't think you're good enough to go out for drill," she said.

"No. I just don't want to!"

"But you haven't even given yourself a chance. If you just come to this introduction meeting you'll change your mind."

"Do I have a choice?" I said. But as usual it was as if the only words that were important were coming out of *her* mouth. I looked at the sky. I knew she hated that. "Is it all right if I go to class now?" I said.

She shot me several darts with her eyes. "Be there," she said, and walked off.

If the truth were known, I wasn't that anxious to get to Creative Writing. I didn't have anything to show Mr. Cecil on my story. I sure wasn't going to let him eyeball the drivel I'd scratched down on the bus.

But I went—and tried to keep a low profile.

"Got anything to show me, Sara?" he said about halfway through class. He slanted casually on the desk next to mine.

I glanced up guiltily from the two sisters being marveled at by the sun and flashed my braces at him. "It's coming," I lied, "but it's not ready for prime-time viewing."

He had fluffy eyebrows that could say more than your average paragraph. He cocked one of them now. He knew.

Why couldn't I get a start on this thing? It haunted me all day, even into the drill team introduction meeting there was no getting out of. Mr. Cecil always said write about what you know, and what did I know better than sisters? I'd had one all my life. Becky had started out leaning over my crib, telling me how to hold my bottle and she hadn't stopped doing the sister thing since—

"That's it!"

Becky hissed a "shh" at me. I hadn't meant to say it out loud, but, then, revelations tend to sneak up behind you.

I gleamed my braces at Becky and pretended to listen to what the drill team faculty advisor was saying about tryouts. When Becky was once again entranced by talk of warm-ups and formations, I soundlessly slid a piece of paper out of my notebook.

But one day the sun didn't shine on the two sisters. There was trouble in paradise. Big Sister Abigail stormed into Little Sister Daphne's room. "Daphne!" she cried, lips trembling, "have you been seeing my beau?" Daphne's hand went to her throat at the sight of the tears glistening in her sister's blue eyes, and her own hazel ones filled.

"Why, Abby, how could you think such a thing of me?" Abigail hung her head.

"Oh, Daphne, I don't think that—not really. I'm sorry. Oh,

dear." And she ran to her sister, throwing her sobbing self into her lap.

"Ugh!"

I clapped my hand over my mouth, but it was too late. Becky's eyes were like two screwdrivers.

Fortunately, the meeting was winding down. I got up to go, and Becky stepped on my heels following me out. There was no point in trying to outrun her.

"Sara," she said tightly as we huffed toward the late bus, "you didn't have to be totally rude and embarrass me in front of the entire drill team."

"I was trying to wr—"

"I know you think I'm being pushy."

It had crossed my mind, but I set my jaw and kept walking.

"I just want you to do at least one thing that's halfway cool before you graduate from high school." Becky stopped at the curb as the bus rounded the turn. She pulled her mouth into an elder sister prune. "I'm only saying this for your own good, Sara. I don't want my little sister being an unpopular geek—and if you keep sitting around burying your head in your notebooks and biting your pen—"

Solemnly I put my hands over my ears and stared at her. She hated that, too. Tossing all of her hair in my face, she flounced onto the bus and flopped down next to Rachel Kelly.

Which was absolutely fine with me. I charged to the back of the bus and sprawled across the seat so nobody could sit next to me. Boring two holes through Becky's shoulder blades, I whipped my pen out of my bag and bit on it—hard. Unpopular geek? Uncool? Fine!

Abigail was sleeping softly with the moonlight shimmering across her face. Daphne crept into the room, knife glinting in that same moonlight as she lifted it over Abigail's head and—

I ripped the pen across the page in one big scratch that tore the words up with it. "*Murder?*" I said out loud. "Get real."

The kid in the seat in front of me looked at me mildly, but I turned my head and stared out through the back window. The whole world was framed by the words EMERGENCY EXIT. That was what I needed, all right. An emergency exit—to get me out of trying out for drill team. To get me out of writing this stupid story. To get me the Sam Hill away from my sister.

She was looking at me over Rachel Kelly's shoulder. Even her eyes said, "Sit up, Sara. You look like an uncool geek."

I hunkered down further. She was my sister. I couldn't hurt her, not even on paper. But I wanted her out of my face.

As soon as we had the table cleared after dinner and I was on my way up to my room to trash everything I'd written and start over, Becky planted herself on the landing, barring my way like a knight ready to slay the Unpopularity Dragon.

"Tryouts start tomorrow," she informed me. "And don't you dare cover your ears, Sara!"

"I wasn't going to cover my ears." I tried to sound weary, like our mother does when we've stretched her patience to the max.

She turned me around by the shoulders.

"Let's go into the backyard and I'll show you some stuff so you won't make a complete fool of yourself at the tryouts."

"Give me a break!" I moved to push past her but she caught my arm.

"You really need to do this, Sara."

"Leave me alone, Becky!" I said. And with the tears coming, I ran up to my room.

By the time I got to class the next day, all I had was three pages of stupidity with X's drawn on them. Mr. Cecil leaned against the wall beside my desk and cocked one of his wonderful eyebrows at them.

"Sara, I've never seen you have so much trouble getting started on a project."

"I guess I'm not going to be the next Danielle Steele after all," I said glumly.

"Let me take a look."

I white-knuckled the pages but he pried them gently out of my hand and read. It was more embarrassing than trying out for the drill team was going to be.

But he didn't laugh. He pulled another desk up close to mine, and spread the pages out in front of us.

"I like your subject," he said. "You were smart to write about—"

"Something you know," I finished for him.

"So let's take a look at where you went wrong."

"I picked up the pen," I said.

He faked a glare. "Start number one has no conflict. You have to have conflict or your story's boring. In fact, without conflict, your *life* is boring."

"Oh, please," I said. "Let me be bored for just one day."

"Start number two has conflict, but it's too easily resolved because the characters are too much alike. That's not real life either."

I could feel my face going into a grimace. "That's for sure."

"Now, start number three—" He arched his eyebrow comically. "*Murder*, Sara?"

I sighed. "So does this just mean I should forget this whole thing and transfer to typing class?"

He gave a dramatic shudder, eyebrows meeting in the middle. "No need to do anything drastic," he said. And then he looked at me softly.

"You're a Christian, aren't you, Sara?"

Oh, now that followed. But I nodded.

"Then you know about Mary and Martha?"

"Mary and Mar—"

"In the Bible."

"Oh. Yeah." I crinkled my nose. "But I don't get it."

"Try to keep up, Sara. We'll be moving a little faster now." He smiled. "Go home after school and read the story of Mary and Martha. It's in Luke. I think that might help you get a handle on your story."

"I can't do it right after school," I said. "I'm supposed to start that drill team tryout thing."

Both his brows shot up to his forehead in sharp points. "You're putting me on."

"No."

"Drill team."

"Yeah."

He shuddered again. "Why?"

"Well—"

"Isn't that a Becky thing?"

"Yeah, but she says I need to do something cool."

He sputtered a guffaw across my papers. "Go home and read Mary and Martha."

There was something in the way he said it that was part of

why I headed for the bus after school instead of for the locker room. Becky was going to condemn me to unpopular geek-hood for the rest of my uncool life. But even as I watched from the back window of the bus when she darted out the front door of the school looking for me, I knew I was doing the right thing.

The Mary and Martha thing was in Luke—chapter ten to be exact. I'd heard it in church, of course. But when I read it this time, it was a different story, maybe because after the first time, I substituted the names Sara and Becky.

At verse forty-one, I screeched on my reading brakes.

Becky, Becky, you are worried and upset about many things, but only one thing is needed. Sara has chosen what is better, and it will not be taken away from her.

Whoa. Becky was Martha, making all the preparations. Doing all the cool, expected things. I mean, after all, somebody had to do them.

But I was Mary. Listening. Observing. Gathering info and writing about it. That was me.

And it wasn't going to be taken away from me.

Scrambling for my book bag, I whipped out my notebook and chewed-up pen.

Daphne looked down from the apple tree where she was perched high on a top branch and tickled her chin with her quill pen. Abigail was running toward her from the house, skirts hiked up above her knees, hair tossed by the wind and her own excitement. Something had happened—a new horse, maybe, or a new beau on the horizon. Daphne sighed. Abigail would expect her to be breathless over it, too, and she wouldn't be, and there would be another argument. It was so hard. They were so—different.

I heard the front door slam.
"Sa-ra!" Becky yelled from below.
I grinned.

"Daphne!" Abigail cried.
"Don't bother me—I'm creating," Daphne said. And she scratched her quill pen across the page.

BUILDING BOXES,
BUILDING TRUST

"We're lost," I said.

"Nah, Shona," he said. "You can still hear everybody."

I didn't hear anything except the trees saying tsk-tsk.

"Adam," I said, "we're lost. C'mon. I think this is the way back."

He slung me over his shoulder caveman style. "Come, woman. We go back to camp."

But when we got to the clearing where only fifteen minutes before, our friends had been devouring the contents of an ice chest, there was nobody there.

"Noah!" Adam yelled. "Staci? Chris?"

"Did they leave us here?"

"No way!" Adam said. "Sean! Josh! Danielle?" He looked at me. "They left us here."

"They're puppy chow!"

"So am I," Adam said. "I'm supposed to be home by five. We'll be lucky to get there before dark walking."

"Especially if you don't put me down."

Adam slid me to the ground, and I reached into the pocket of my Levis for a quarter. "We'll just hike to the store and call my dad."

"Is he going to kill you?"

"Why should he?" I said. "I haven't done anything wrong."

"Just to be on the safe side, Shon," he said, "let's call *my* dad."

* * * * *

My wife was out of town. My daughter Shona was off in the woods with a bunch of kids. And I was pacing the kitchen floor.

I'd paced a track in the carpeting the day she was born. This was the first time since that she'd given me reason to do it again.

I hadn't liked the idea of her going off on a picnic—eight kids in the woods with maybe enough sense among them to operate the pop tops on the soda cans.

But I'd said she could go because I couldn't think of a reason not to let her other than, "I'm afraid you're going to get up there in the woods and one thing's going to lead to another and boys being what they are, especially these days, all four of them are going to jump you and you'll come back diseased, pregnant, drunk, drugged up—"

I *had* said she had to be home by four. It was 4:30. I'd been pacing since three. I took two more turns past the stove before the front door opened and there she was.

Her face was flushed, her eyes sparkled, and she was the image of her mother when I'd fallen in love with her at nineteen.

"Where have you been?" I said.

"I am never going anywhere with those banana brains again! Daddy, do you know what they did to us?"

"Where have you been?" I said again.

"Adam and I went off for a walk—"

"You left the rest of the group?"

"Just for a couple of minutes—"

"This wasn't supposed to be a single date."

"We were gone fifteen minutes! When we got back, they'd left us. I'm calling Staci—"

"I'm talking to you!"

She froze, her hand halfway to the phone, and stared at me with surprised eyes.

"I don't like this, Shona," I said. I could feel my stomach bunching up. "The first time I let you go off without adult supervision and you blow it."

"I couldn't help it if they took off!"

"You should never have left the group in the first place. I trusted you to keep this a friendly group thing."

Shona's voice was teetering. "They were having a *burping* contest and it was disgusting, so I asked Adam to go for a walk with me."

"You're inviting trouble when you do something like that, Shona."

"Daddy—"

"You don't need to be out with boys when it's obvious you don't know how they operate."

"You mean I'm grounded?"

If I'd thought she looked surprised before, she was incredulous now.

"I'm *grounded?*" she said again. "But I didn't do anything wrong!"

"Two weeks," I said.

With a swish of Levis she ran out of the kitchen, and I leaned heavily on the counter. I knew I was right—but I felt so old.

* * * * *

I cried that night until my eyes were swollen into red slits. And after Dad and I sat silently in church together the next morning, I went home and cried some more. It wasn't just that I wouldn't get to hang out with Adam or the rest of my friends for two weeks. It was the unfairness of it. I hadn't done anything wrong. I'd thought Dad would be *proud* of me for being able to get myself home.

Breathing in hiccups, I tore down the hiking picture of us from my bulletin board.

Daddy's little girl. I'd been that since—forever.

And I'd thought that when I was a teenager we'd be *friends*. I'd pictured him watching football with my boyfriends and pinning corsages on me and saying sweet, protective things like, "Do you have some mad money with you? Do you need more?"

Not accusing me of deliberately sneaking off into the woods to make out with a guy, not totally distrusting me when there was no reason to.

I picked up the backpack he'd bought me last summer and threw it against the bookshelves he'd built for my room.

The phone rang, and for the first three rings I didn't answer it. Dad was in the basement in his workshop with the power tools grinding. If he missed an important phone call because he couldn't hear the phone, tough. *I* wasn't supposed to have any contact with the outside world.

I picked it up anyway, out of spite. It was Adam.

"Are you mad at me?" he said. "You didn't even look at me this morning."

"I'm not allowed to," I said.

"Huh?"

"Nothing. I'm not mad at *you.*"

"He's mad, huh, your dad?"

"Yeah."

"Listen—" I could almost see him massacring the phone cord in agony. "Do you want me to talk to him?"

I don't know what people who have been in love a lot call it, but I call it a surge. You know, that feeling you get when somebody you like a lot does something so cool you just want to hug them? Shy, mumble-to-the-floor Adam volunteering to defend me to my father. I loved him for that.

"I want to see you!" I said. "Meet me at the school."

"But—won't your dad—"

"I don't care," I said. "Meet me!"

* * * * *

Whenever I have to duke it out with myself over something, I start a building project—a shelf, a wooden duck, a house— anything. The tools grinding and the sawdust flying and the way I whistle through my teeth when I work helps me get things straight in my mind. If you follow the rules in carpentry the job turns out right. It doesn't work out that way in raising kids.

So I went down to the basement right after church and started on a cedar chest for Shona. I'd gotten the idea during the service to give it to her for her birthday and explain to her that she could collect stuff in it for when she was married some- day—all grown-up. But she wasn't grown-up now. She wasn't ready for guys and freedom and the responsibilities of dating.

I don't even remember turning on the table saw or picking up the cedar. I hardly had to think about what I was doing when it came to wood, I'd done it for so long.

That's when you get into trouble—when you think you're beyond mistakes. I don't know even now how my hand slipped, how it went through the saw, how the workshop walls got splattered with blood and I ended up sagged against the table, groping for my senses.

"Shona!" I heard myself cry. But the saw was still running, and my voice was thready. She couldn't hear me and I had to make her hear me. I was sure I'd cut my hand off.

I slid my other hand down the side of the table and flipped off the saw. The floor careened crazily and tilted against my head. I tried to call Shona again, but the blackness cut me off.

* * * * *

The big saw was gnashing its teeth in the basement. There was no way my dad could've heard me open the front door, but the minute my hand touched the doorknob, the saw stopped.

I froze, heart slamming against my rib cage, and a pang ran through me—like what you feel when a puppy whimpers. I listened. There was nothing.

Still, I tiptoed through the kitchen to the top of the basement steps. Dad always whistled through his teeth when he was building something. But it was quiet.

If I called to him, there would go all possibility of getting out the front door. But this was so strange—

"Dad?"

I knew before I reached the bottom I was going to find him on the floor.

"Daddy!" I screamed.

I put one hand on my mouth to keep from gagging. My

dad's hand was sliced halfway through and dangled from his wrist. All I could think about was people slashing their wrists. People *died* from slashing their wrists.

I slipped through the blood and got to the phone in the kitchen. I think someone on the other end of 911 said they'd be right there. Towels, I thought. That's how you put bodies back together. First aid. Biology class. It all tangled in my brain like the mass of things that were now severed from my father's hand. I grabbed every towel in the closet and flew down the stairs.

His hand was limp and oozing, and with my teeth digging into my bottom lip I pushed it back to its wrist and wrapped it in all the towels, just to get the blood to go away.

"It'll be OK, Daddy," I kept saying. "I'm wrapping it up. They're coming. Don't die. Please don't die."

I was covering him with a picnic blanket when the paramedics came. One of them took me by the arm. "Come on, let me help you upstairs," he said. "You don't need to see all this blood."

"I'm already wearing it," I said. "It's my dad's."

* * * * *

Her face and sweater were soaked in blood when I opened my eyes in the emergency room. I tried to come up off the table.

"It's OK, Mr. Cummings," a male voice said. "You're in the hospital. You've had an accident."

"Shona—were you hurt?" I said crazily.

My beautiful, puffy-eyed daughter put her hand on my face. "That's *your* blood, Daddy. They're taking you to surgery. They're going to try to save your hand."

"Chances are good, Mr. Cummings," the guy voice said. "Only because your daughter has her act together."

The light above me swayed, and I strained to keep my eyes open. "I love you, Baby," I wanted to say to her. I think it came out "alobobaba."

But she knew, and she kissed me on the forehead.

As they slid the table toward the door, I felt like a boy—vulnerable and out of control.

Shona was walking beside me. Now *she* looked old, so very old.

* * * * *

"Mom's already on a flight home," I told him. "She isn't going to let you play with your toys anymore."

Dad half-smiled and looked up at the IV. "This has to be the stupidest thing I ever did. I shouldn't have been working with power tools in that frame of mind."

"That was my fault, Daddy," I said.

"No—it's your 'fault' I'm still alive."

"But you don't know—" I stopped. While he'd been fighting for his life in surgery, I'd been fighting with my guilt. What if I *had* sneaked out? What if I hadn't been there for him? The guilt was choking me now, and if I didn't get it out, *I* was going to die.

Seeing him lying there, though, with the first tears I'd ever seen in his eyes, I couldn't tell him.

"I'm sorry about yesterday," he said. "I can see I should've given you more credit."

"Maybe *that* time," I said. "But I *can* be pretty clueless."

A tear leaked out onto his cheek as he smiled with the

other half. "Looks like we need to help each *other* with that one," he said.

I had one of those surges then. You know—the ones that happen when someone you really like does something cool—and you want to hug them?

MOVE OVER, MOM

"Good-bye, Boston," I said through the rear window of Joan's Miata. "Keep growing those great shoulders."

From the driver's seat Joan laughed softly, something I was going to have to learn to do if I was going to be anything like her. My guffaw could disrupt hibernation.

"So you're sticking to your theory that to be a bellhop in Boston you have to have great shoulders?" Joan said.

"All of ours did. Of course, it *was* the Park Plaza. Maybe the swankier the hotel, the bigger the shoulders. Whoa—I wonder what the guys are like at the Ritz Carlton!"

Joan squeezed my hand. "Shelly, you are a pure delight. Thank you for sharing this weekend with me."

I just grinned back at her. I'd already told her eight hundred times since Friday night how much I appreciated all she was doing for me. In the three short weeks since she'd come up to me in church and asked if I wanted to enter a young models' contest for the department store chain she worked for, I'd found nooks and crannies in my life I didn't even know were there—and she'd uncovered most of them for me. Who knew my hair could look like this, or my nails? Who knew I'd learn how to walk like I *wasn't* going from the pitcher's mound to center field—or that I'd break into the finals and get to spend a weekend in Boston with Joan—or that I'd be chosen for a photo shoot for the store's sale catalog? As my brother Kevin would say, go figure!

"My mom's going to be so jazzed," I said.

"You two are really close, aren't you?"

"Oh yeah. My dad died when I was seven and the boys were just babies, so we've always been like friends."

Joan shook her head sympathetically. "It must have been hard for you, growing up without a father."

"In some ways, yeah." I snickered. "But my mom's a better dad than most fathers I know. She taught all three of us how to pitch a softball and have a decent backhand. You should see her out on the ice in January, shoveling off the snow so we can play hockey. She coaches my softball team."

"I know. Michelle's an amazing woman," Joan said.

"But, then, so are you." I looked down in amazement at my hands. "Who else could've made *these* nails looks like *this?*"

"Anytime you need anything, I'm around," she said.

I pretty much keep to myself, and mostly I just talk to my mom when it comes to the really important stuff. But as I looked back for one more glimpse of Boston before we headed up the coast, I thought, cool—I've gotten three new things this weekend: new hair, new nails, and a new friend.

The closer we got to home the more hyper I got, till by the time Joan pulled into our driveway I was headed up the front walk, bags trailing behind me, news bubbling out of my mouth before Mom even met me at the door. Somewhere between "It was so totally cool" and "I brought all of you guys presents," Joan waved and took off in her Miata with me shouting, "I'll call you tomorrow."

Mom corralled Kevin and Patrick to help us lug the bags upstairs.

"What'd you do to your hair?" Kevin said. "You look like a schnauzer."

"Wow, how'd you grow your nails so long?" Patrick said.

"They're fakes until I can grow my own out."

"You're going to catch a softball with those talons?" Mom said.

"I guess I'll find out tomorrow," I said. "Oh, Mom, it was the most awesome weekend. I had lobster at Legal Seafood."

"Aw, man, no fair!" Patrick wailed.

"Joan is so cool. We stayed up till one in the morning talking. She had a suite for us, but mostly I was in her room jacking my jaws."

"A suite?" Kevin said. "Dude, she must be rich."

"All right, everybody hit the showers," Mom said. "Tomorrow's a school day."

Kevin and Patrick trailed off moaning. I grabbed Mom in a hug. "I'm too excited to sleep. I have so much to tell you."

She peeled my arms from around her neck. "It'll keep. You have practice after school. Our first game's Saturday. You didn't make any plans, did you?"

I stared at her. "Of course not. I checked the schedule before I said I'd do the photo shoot. It's cool."

"Put your dirty clothes in the laundry room," she said. And she closed the door behind her.

I felt like a popped balloon. My mom never did that. She'd listened to every word I'd said since ma-ma and da-da. But she'd just blown me off. My own mother had just blown me off.

I went to the mirror and scrunched my new do with my fingers. Don't brush it, Joan had said. Just scrunch.

That was it, of course. Mom hated the hair, the nails, the whole thing. She wanted me to ski in the Olympics or become a tennis pro. I smiled at the new me in the mirror. No problem. Joan had assured me I could do both, and Mom would see that, and everything would be cool. I looked ruefully at my shiny red claws. But the jury was still out on how well these puppies were going to do in a softball mitt.

They didn't do well. By Tuesday after practice, three of them had bitten the dust. Joan laughed, softly, on the phone and told me to come on over.

I rode my bike to her house after I showered. There was no time to scrunch my wet hair, but she just gave me a hug when I arrived and broke out the mineral water and carrot sticks and went to work on my nails.

"I've missed you," she said. "By the way, I was at a luncheon at the Holiday Inn here in town today. The bellhops look like pencils."

"I told you!"

"So how's your life?"

I'd never really thought of myself as having a "life," but you couldn't have proven it by the twenty minutes worth of conversation that came pouring out of my mouth. I hadn't talked that much since Sunday. And it felt good to have someone to talk to. My mother had been strangely quiet since I'd gotten home from Boston. When I'd asked her if I could come over to Joan's, she'd given a grunt which I'd translated as a halfhearted yes.

"How's your mom?" Joan asked when she could get a word in. It didn't even surprise me that she seemed to be reading my mind now.

"Grumpy," I said.

Joan's perfectly tweezed eyebrows shot up. "I imagine she has the right to get cranky once in awhile, raising three active kids all by herself."

"Yeah, but that's her whole life. She always says she loves being a mom."

"That doesn't mean she doesn't have her bad days. I loved modeling, too, but there were times when I wanted to stick my tongue out at the camera. She's human."

I looked at Joan in awe. Talk about an amazing woman.

I rode up our driveway feeling like everything was in the right slot once more. But it all came sliding out again the minute I opened the back door.

"Dinner is on the table," Mom said, in lieu of "hello."

"I didn't have a dinner chore tonight. I checked."

She sniffed. "Wash your hands."

"I can't. The glue isn't all the way dry."

"You know, I'm getting a little tired of the world revolving around your fingernails."

"That isn't fair, Mom! Joan just said—"

"And I'm getting *more* than tired of hearing what 'Joan said.'"

"Well, I'm not! Right now, she's a whole lot more understanding about my life than you are!"

The minute the words crossed my lips, I was sorry I'd spit them at her.

Not only because I could see the hurt stinging in her eyes. Not only because what I'd said wasn't even true. But because for the first time it dawned on me that she didn't care if I modeled clothes or shot baskets or slung hash. She just thought I liked Joan better than I liked her.

And after what I'd just said, what else could she think?

But she didn't give me a chance to say I was sorry. She just pointed to the door, and I went up to my room. On the way, I found myself thinking, "Joan would've talked it out with me." But a week before, so would Mom.

For the next few days, we didn't say much to each other beyond, "Have you done your homework?" and "Yes, ma'am." Even at practice our conversations sounded like "Watch your follow-through." "OK." The silences in between were deafening.

By Saturday's game I could barely think about anything except how miserable I was. The only thing that cheered me up was seeing Joan in the stands. She looked strangely out of place in her designer warm-up suit, but her smile and wave lifted the sag.

"Have a good game, Shelly," a husky voice said behind me.

"Thanks, Mom," I said, to my shoe.

But I didn't have a good game. I struck out in the top of the first inning and missed a fly ball in the bottom. I had no concentration. When everybody else was yelling, "Go for third!" I was thinking, "Mom, this is stupid. Why can't you talk to me?"

That's probably why I forgot to put on a batting helmet and strolled up to the plate just as Tish Rogowski was flinging her bat to take off for first base. That's probably why I got hit in the head with it.

Being unconscious is a weird thing. It isn't like going to sleep—it's like going away for a very long time. When I came back I could just make out Mom's very blurry face close to mine.

"Shelly! Shelly, can you hear me, Honey?"

I tried to nod, and I left again.

When I returned the next time I wondered vaguely why Patrick had "Rescue 911" turned up so loud. Only later did Mom tell me I'd been in an ambulance with the siren blaring.

When I really came back for good, we were in the emergency room. Mom was pulling the gown up over my chest and shaking her head. "Men," she said. "They never put anything back where it belongs."

"Did I have my chest exposed to the whole world?" I said.

"Just the whole hospital. But I took care of it."

"Thanks," I said.

I had a concussion, but they determined there was no brain damage. Mom said Kevin would argue with that diagnosis. But they did insist that I spend the night in the hospital for observation. And I insisted that Mom stay with me.

"You want me to?" she said. There was something almost childlike in the tears in her eyes.

"I'm not staying here without you," I said.

The doctor told her to wake me up every two hours to be sure I was sleeping normally and hadn't lapsed into unconsciousness again. At the four o'clock call, I was wide awake.

"Tell me a Bible story, Mom."

"What?"

"Remember how you used to tell us stories from the Bible to put us to sleep when we were little?"

"I remember, but I didn't think you did."

"It was my favorite part of being a little kid."

Mom stroked my forehead, and I watched her face. It was beautiful. She could have been a model herself.

"OK, here's one I've been thinking about," she said. "Once upon a time, God had two children—Adam and Eve, and they had two kids. God told them that the natural thing was going to be for their boys to leave them and make their own lives. What He didn't say was how hard it was going to be for the parents to let go when the kids made other adult friends and started—leaving." She had tears in her eyes but her husky voice was steady. "It's healthy for you to have a friend like Joan. She's incredible. Did you know she called the ambulance and got the team calmed down and took the boys home? The last time I talked to her, she was making them homemade pizza. She can teach you so many things I can't. What do I know about eyeliner and pantyhose?"

"But she can never take your place, Mom. I never even thought she could."

"I know that now. But jealousy can take good sense and twist it beyond recognition."

We were quiet for a minute. Then I said, "In that story, does God say the kid gets to be a brat when she's 'leaving'?"

Mom guffawed, the way I do. "No!" she said.

"I really wasn't thinking about your feelings when I was going on about how wonderful Joan was and stuff."

I think Mom nodded; I'm not sure. I was getting pretty drowsy and the pillow was coming up around the sides of my face. I think I said "I'm sorry I was hateful," although I'm not sure of that, either. But it doesn't really matter, because she knew. Moms know that stuff.

And only moms.

THE FAMILY TWINKLE

"Tamara, are you planning to pout the entire time?" my mother said to me from the front seat.

"Do I have to stop this car?" My father's eyes twinkled at me in the rearview mirror. "Leave her alone, Maggie," he said quietly to my mother.

It was cool that my father understood, but as I glared miserably at the Georgia pines whipping past me outside the rental car, I didn't feel much better. With each passing swamp that took us further from Michigan—and Jeff—I just got gloomier.

"I don't want you sulking around Grandma Lou," my mother couldn't resist saying. "This is her last Christmas in her own house before she moves into the retirement home and we all want this to be a real celebration for our family."

"Does Tammy have to enjoy it?" my father teased.

I snorted silently. I wasn't planning on enjoying anything this Christmas that didn't have to do with Jeff and my friends. I'd had it with "family" on this trip already.

"Well," Mom said, just before Dad caught her in a one-armed headlock, "just be sure your great-grandmother doesn't know you're brooding."

"Better put a bag over your head, Tam," Dad said.

I hadn't been to Waycross, Georgia, since I was six, and none of the white-columned houses and funky little grocery stores looked familiar. Even when we drove up to Grandma

Lou's there was no nostalgia for me. I just wanted to be in Michigan putting on my ice skates—with Jeff.

What seemed like forty-seven children belched from the front door when we drove up.

"Is that Bill's little Kelsey?" my mother said. "Has she grown!"

How she could tell one kid from another was beyond me. I stood by the car as they danced around like banshees.

The grown-ups gathered on the porch as if the Queen Mother were about to appear. When Grandma Lou did emerge through the screen door, I had to look twice. Ten years is a long time when a person is going from eighty to ninety. This wizened lady with the thinning snowy hair bore almost no resemblance to the woman who'd been riding horses and hurling hay bales the last time I was there. Reluctantly I approached the porch to give my duty hug.

"Here's our Tammy," Dad said.

"I can see that," Grandma Lou scolded him. She surveyed me out of her pecan brown face and said, "You'll be wanting your own room."

I was surprised—but grateful. The first thing I did in there was write a letter to Jeff. I told him I didn't know how I was going to be able to stand two weeks away from him and all the kids we hung out with.

I didn't want my mom to know I was already writing him, so I couldn't ask her for a stamp. Then a memory popped in. I'd helped Grandma Lou mail her bills once, and I'd been thrilled as a kid to find out that the stamps were in a secret compartment in her desk in the library.

The other members of our enormous family were all in the

kitchen presumably feasting on Grandma Lou's famous fruit-cake that I was supposed to love. They were making too much noise to hear me slip into the library and close the door.

There was definitely a smell in there—I remembered that, too. It was a combination of honeysuckle and old books and lemon furniture polish. The scent slowed me down for a minute. It was so definitely *her*.

I opened the front of the cherry desk, and as I moved several slim leather volumes aside one fell open. The smell wafted from it as I looked closer at the perfect curlicues of writing on its pages.

"Today, I met a boy—" said the violet ink.

"Ah, so you've found my journals."

I jerked back my hand and let the book fall to the rug. Grandma Lou leaned over to pick it up.

"I've left these to you in my will," she said. "But you're going to have to wait until I die to read them. I'm not finished with them yet."

There was a familiar twinkle in her eye as she laid the journal carefully back in the desk.

I knew my face was the color of her poinsettias, and I groped for something—anything—to say.

"I was actually looking for a stamp—"

"Ah." Her fingers deftly pushed open the secret compartment. "Writing a love letter?" she said, handing me a 32-center.

"Well—yeah."

"I thought you had that look about you," she said. "Well, for heaven sakes, why don't you call him?"

"Long distance? From here?"

She twinkled at me again. "We've had phones here for several years."

"I didn't mean—"

"Call him," she said. Then she slipped out.

My fingers shook as I dialed Jeff's number, but I could have saved myself the trouble. The conversation went something like this:

"Jeff? Hi!"

"Tammy?"

"Yes! I'm calling from Georgia! Can you stand it! I miss you—"

"Listen, Tam, can you call me back? We're just going out the door to go—Hey, Mike, knock it off, I'm comin'! Can you call me back?"

"I miss you."

"Yeah, me too—I'm comin', already! Gotta go, Tam."

I was shredding the letter when Grandma Lou reappeared with a loaded tea tray.

"He blew you off, eh?" she said.

I couldn't help exploding out a startled laugh.

"I watch television," Grandma Lou said. She twinkled her eyes softly. "God made boys to be slower growing up. He must have had his reasons—I don't know—but young men that age sure don't know how to be in love yet like we women want them to. Don't you fret."

Something about her made it hard *to* "fret." It was the twinkle, and now I knew where I'd seen it before.

"I just noticed how much my dad looks like you," I said.

"And you look like him, so what does that tell you?" She chuckled. "Too bad God doesn't let you pick your relatives."

I nestled back with my tea into a brocade chair I now remembered dated back to the Civil War.

"What else do you know about boys?" I said.

She spent the rest of the afternoon telling me, while I laughed until I had tears collecting at the corners of my eyes.

"This is no laughing matter!" she said. But her eyes twinkled at me, and mine twinkled back.

After the third time a granddaughter-in-law peeked into the library, Grandma Lou stood up. "They think it's my naptime," she said.

I looked up at her shyly. "You've done so much for me this afternoon," I said. "Is there something I can do—I mean, to help you?"

She didn't even have to think about it. "Yes! Keep your parents and the rest of my grown-up grandchildren out of my hair." She winked. "What there is left of it."

There was no snow on Christmas morning, of course, but as I pulled back the lace curtains I decided I kind of liked the Georgia pines after all.

"Come on, Tammy!" said my little cousin Sarah—or Samantha—or Tabitha—one of them. "It's time to open presents!"

My mother would've been proud of me: I only thought about Jeff once—and immediately discarded the idea that he would be swooning over the romantic gift I'd left for him to open. The rest of the time I was in stitches over it all. The little kids. The mountains of wrapping paper. The fruitcake nobody ate. The laughter of four generations. It was kind of wonderful.

But the best part came when I found my package from

Grandma Lou. Inside were two slim leather journals. One was blank.

"For writing about all the young men who will stumble clumsily through your life," she'd written on the inside. "God bless you—and them."

The other was filled with elegant violet writing and the smell of her.

"A piece of our family," she penned. "Families are powerful. That's why Jesus was born into one."

I looked up to find her winking at me.

"I decided not to wait until I die," she said.

And I knew in a way, she never really *would* die. She'd be leaving the twinkle behind.

GUYS AND OTHER THINGS

THAT FRY YOUR BRAINS

DREAM WEAVER

A shaft of silver light shot across the stage and glittered it all to life—his shimmering silk shirt, his gleaming guitar, his penetrating eyes. Behind me the crowd screamed for him to sing to us and tell us how it was with his magic words. But I didn't join them. I couldn't. I could only gaze in silence—because there was a connection between him and me, something only he and I could feel and understand. Then, with a dazzling flash he turned—and I knew he felt it, too. The roar faded behind me as Eric Champion's eyes and mine locked. All I could hear were the clear, silver words he spoke from the stage to me—only me—

"Corinna. Corinna Stanley!"

A freckled hand waved across my computer screen. Slowly I looked up.

"Anyone home here?" Mr. Walls said.

"Yes, sir," I said.

He looked curiously at my screen, from which the same green paragraph glared back that had been there fifteen minutes ago when we'd started the assignment.

"I think you're seeing something I'm not," he said. "Nobody's eyes could get that big over capitalization."

"Ooh!" Kenny Allan said from the next monitor. "Capital R—ooh!"

Across the aisle, Holly giggled.

That's when my face started to burn. Mr. Walls could humiliate me in front of the class. He was the teacher—it was in his contract. And Kenny Allan could make fun of me into eternity. He was a jerk, and that was in *his* contract. But when *Holly* laughed—

She'd been my best friend since Barbie doll days—until recently, when anything a cute guy said took priority over everything else, including my feelings. When Holly laughed at my expense, I wanted to cry all over my disk drive.

The bell rang. That's how I'm reassured God really loves me—when the bell rings at times like that.

Holly gathered up her books and I dove for mine, knocking *Addison-Wesley Mathematics* gracefully to the floor in a splash of pages. I followed it under the table.

"Whoa, Corinna, before you submerge," Mr. Walls said.

"Yes, sir," I said.

I pulled my head out and banged both it and my knee getting into the chair.

"You OK?" he said.

"Sure—I won't even get a bruise—I do that all the time—"

"How do you explain the fact that I called on you twice today and you didn't even hear me?"

"I didn't?"

"Evidently not—unless you call glazed eyes and a lip hanging to your knees a response."

At that point my eyes dropped to my knees, too. I could never remember being "yelled at" by a teacher in my whole eight years of school, and it was definitely polishing off an already-trashed morning.

"It looks like we have some daydreaming going on here," Mr. Walls said.

My face jerked up guiltily.

"That has its place, but this isn't it." He smeared a freckled hand across his face. "I want to see you firmly planted in the real world tomorrow, or I think your folks and I will need to have a little chat."

My eyes went all the way to the floor this time, and they stayed there as I made my way to the door. I'd sure never had a teacher call my parents.

"Cory—you OK?"

I looked up, and Holly was walking beside me. The way her feathery brows were knit in concern—I decided to forget she'd just betrayed me to the male world.

"I just got yelled at by Mr. Walls," I said.

"You?"

"If I don't start paying attention in class he's going to call my parents."

"They'll kill you!"

"Du-uh!"

Holly closed her hand over my arm. "Don't worry. You'll get it together. I'll help you."

A smile sprawled over my face. "You want to sit together at lunch?"

She was going to say yes—I know she was. But then we both smelled it—a male presence reeking of Polo. I turned around, and Lance Hendrix was leering into Holly's face. He slipped a note into her hand and took off.

"What was that all about?" I said.

But I might as well have asked in Turkish. Holly gazed at

the note, giggled, looked at it again, giggled, and took off backward down the hall.

"See you fifth period?" she said. "I gotta go and—well, I've just gotta go!"

With one more giggle she was history. I shrugged, just in case anybody was watching, and quickly found a corner of the courtyard. It was OK. I could eat my bologna sandwich and read the article about Eric Champion in the magazine I'd gotten yesterday. I'd read it already, actually, but there were always those little details that slipped by you the first four times—

I slid my pen and pad from my pocket and watched him as he paced around his dressing room.

"Mr. Champion," I said calmly, "there's no need to be nervous. I just have a few brief questions. Could we start with your leaving your home to go to Columbus, Georgia, just because your mother said the Lord told her you should go?"

His eyebrows arched up sharply. "How did you know about that?"

"I've done my homework," I said.

"You don't believe God directs our lives like that?"

It was my turn to arch my brow. "Of course!" I said. "I'm a Christian, too, Mr. Champion. I don't know who else would direct our lives."

His face softened, and slowly he came to sit beside me. "Put that pen down," he said huskily. "Let's get to know each other as people." He looked into my eyes. "Hasn't anyone told you—"

—there's a fire drill!"

For a second I didn't recognize Mr. Walls' freckled face —

until he said, "Hasn't anyone told you there's a fire drill, young lady! Get yourself up and get out of here!"

I looked around. The courtyard was empty, and the alarm was blaring in obnoxious blasts. Mr. Walls reached his hand down and pulled me up. "You'd better stay with me," he said. "I don't want you wandering into the men's room or something."

If there had actually been a fire in the building my face couldn't have burned any hotter—or so I thought until we got outside and Mr. Walls made me stand next to him through the entire drill. Then my skin temperature went up twenty degrees.

"Why does Corinna Stanley have a personal escort to the fire drill?" a guy said behind me. I sniffed. It was Lance.

"She's weird," another guy said. I cringed. It was Kenny.

"Now you guys leave her alone," a third person said. I froze. That was Holly.

And then she laughed. They said I was weird, and my best friend laughed with them. I clutched my backpack up against me and prayed for the alarm to stop so I could tear out of there. She thought I was weird, too, then, because I didn't chase boys and I still wanted my best friend and my magazines and my happy little life. Maybe she was right. Maybe I was a total geek.

That night those same thoughts were still circling my brain like planes that would never land when my dad knocked on my door.

"Come on in," I said, and closed the Eric Champion article I had open in my lap. But Dad saw the other stuff as soon as he walked in—the three Eric Champion posters and the letter he'd written me back when I'd sent him fan mail and the words to "Generation of Right" I'd typed in huge letters on the computer at school all displayed on my walls.

"What is this, a shrine?" he said. "Who is this character?"

"He's a Christian pop singer, Dad," I said, trying to keep the Dad-come-on-get-real tone out of my voice. "I like him."

"Like him? Have you promised to give him your firstborn child?"

"Da-ad!"

"I'm just giving you a hard time." He nodded at the chair layered with clothes. "Is it OK if I sit down?"

"Sure," I said. I pulled my knees up to my chin. It was going to come any minute—the lecture about Mr. Walls, and me being so far out there I missed an entire fire drill.

But Dad looked up at my walls again and chuckled.

"Twiggy," he said.

"Huh?" I said.

"You're a slacker with this Champion cat, compared to what I was with Twiggy. You can't even compete with your old man until you have every *inch* of these walls not just covered but *obliterated* with propaganda."

"Uh, Dad—what are you talking about?"

"When I was about your age—"

Oh. The when-I-was-thirteen-I-walked-ten-miles-in-the-snow thing.

"—my room looked like a temple to Twiggy."

"Who's Twiggy?"

Dad bugged his eyes out at me. "Cory, come on, get *real*, babe! Twiggy was only *the* hottest thing in the '60s."

"What did she do—sing?"

"No, she didn't do anything. She was a model."

"Oh."

"And not just any model. She weighed about eighty pounds. Turn her sideways and she disappeared completely."

"Was she anorexic?"

"I don't think we had that back then. No, I think she was just skinny. But her eyes—Cor, she had eyes that were to die for, and she made them look even bigger with this hairdo she wore—kind of short, but long here, and down straight."

I stuffed a pillow in front of my mouth to keep from guffawing. I'd never seen my dad describe a hairstyle before. He looked like he was giving directions to the interstate.

"But I was in love with her," he was saying. "Oh man, I couldn't *think* about anything else. I'd be taking an algebra test and realize I'd just written 'X-3 = Twiggy.'"

I couldn't help myself then. I howled.

"Oh, it gets better," he said. "I got myself a paper route so I could save the money to fly to London to see her in person. At ten bucks a week it would've taken me until—" he glanced at his watch—"just about now."

I stopped laughing. This was starting to sound way too familiar.

"Why'd you have such a crush on this chick?" I said.

"Why *her* in particular I couldn't tell you. I look at old pictures of her now and I think she looked like she just returned from Ethiopia. But why a crush—I guess that's just normal."

He wiggled his eyebrows at me. I shrugged.

"And part of it, too, was that I was kind of 'different' back then. You know, all the other guys were dying to get their driver's licenses and play high school ball and date girls and I could've cared less. I mean, I still kind of wanted to pretend we were space invaders."

"Dad—you were a geek!"

"Exactly. So my little thing with Twiggy was a safe way to fall in love and still be a kid."

I looked up. Eric was staring out of his poster, smiling and making me feel like the cutest chick since—Twiggy.

"Dad?" I said.

He pulled himself back from Twiggy memories. "Yeah?"

"Do you think I'm a geek?"

He didn't immediately say, "Are you kidding? Of course not!" I kind of loved him for that. Instead, he leaned back and surveyed me carefully.

"Do you write Eric Champion's name on all your note-books?" he said.

"Well—yeah," I said.

"Do you daydream that he finds you different from every other girl he's ever met?"

I shrugged. "Kind of."

"And do you tell your friends you can't go places with them because you're waiting for a phone call from him?"

"Da-ad! No!"

"Two out of three." He shook his head. "Nah. You're not a geek—not like your old man."

I settled back into my pillows.

"Nope—I think you're perfectly normal. Problem with being normal, though, is it sometimes gets in the way of you doing the things you're supposed to do—little stuff like school-work. You know what I'm saying?"

I nodded slowly. Here it came.

But he didn't say anything. I couldn't stand it.

"Did Mr. Walls call you?" I said.

"Yeah," he said. "I don't think he ever had a crush on Twiggy." He got up and kissed me on the forehead. "Homework now. And prayers. And don't think about Eric while operating heavy machinery, OK?"

As he closed my door behind him, I wanted to call him back and tell him about Holly and feeling like a sixth finger and all those things. But I didn't. I figured he already knew.

Sighing, I picked up *Addison-Wesley Mathematics*. Before I attacked the first problem, though, I leaned back into the pillows and closed my eyes.

Eric sat in front of me and pulled my hands into his. "Something's on your mind, Corinna," he said.

I nodded slowly. "Something is. Eric—our relationship—I'm afraid it's starting to be more than I'd intended it to be. I'm so wrapped up in you and in us, I can't concentrate on the things I'm supposed to be doing—my career, my studies, my spiritual life."

He put his finger to my lips. "You don't have to say anything else, Corinna," he said. "I understand. Don't forget, I was thirteen once myself."

Grateful tears filled my eyes.

"Whatever you have to do, you know I'll understand," he said. "But please always remember that you're different from any girl I've ever met."

I laughed softly. "I know," I said. "I'm two-thirds geek."

RETURN TO BETHANY FIELDS

"Samuel, I gotta tell you something."

"What?"

"That last pass you made? That was really using your head."

Sam stared. "Kiffany."

"What?"

"Honey, I gotta tell *you* something. That is the *oldest* joke in soccer. The *oldest! And* the most lame!"

I squealed, a habit I'd picked up since I'd been going out with Sam, and kept running. We must've looked like two escapees from the psychiatric ward: Kiffany Cameron, the only girl on the soccer team, and Sam Boscovich, the only guy in school who could bake peanut butter cookies for his girlfriend and still walk out of most locker rooms with his ego intact. We were the off-the-wall couple of the year. It was like our shining moment in time.

My arm was almost ripped out of the socket by the time we got to Jake's. One of the neat things about living in a small town is that there's still a hangout like you see on reruns of *Happy Days*. The drawback is everybody there knows what's going on in your life before *you* do. Lindy was dragging me off to the restroom instantly. I was lucky to have an arm left at all.

"Kiffie, we have to talk," she said when I was locked in the bathroom massaging my bicep.

"What was my first clue?"

"You are *not* going to believe who moved back here."

"I didn't know anybody left," I said. "Do you have a brush?"

"Here—for Pete's sake, yes—you look like you just had a run-in with a lawn mower."

"So who moved back here? Wait—Matt Damon."

"Did he live here? No—Kiffie, *listen* to me. This is *important*."

I pulled the brush through my recently mowed head and laughed. "Who, Lindy?"

"Bethany Fields."

"Be still, my heart. Who's Bethany F—" I stopped, brush in mid-snarl, and watched Lindy nod solemnly. "She's Sam's old—"

"—girlfriend. The last one he had until you moved here." Lindy's eyes got big and sincere. "They were totally an item. They were in youth group together just like you two. She didn't play soccer, but she never missed a game of his. He could barely brush his teeth without her beside him. They were like Siamese twins—"

"Lindy—"

"—always holding hands. It's hard to carry a cafeteria tray when you're holding hands, but they—"

"I get the picture." I tossed the brush in the sink.

"Kiffie, I'm sorry. I didn't mean to—"

"Rub my face in it?"

Miserably I hoisted myself up onto the counter. Lindy hoisted beside me.

"I thought you needed to know before the little vixen tried to *really* move back in," she said. "Are you going to be OK with this?"

I didn't answer her. In about seven seconds I'd gone from shining all over to bearing a close resemblance to a California raisin. I started to climb off the counter, but I stopped and searched the mirror. "Do I really look like I combed my hair with a lawn mower?"

I'd never met Bethany, although I'd heard enough about her. People tended to use words like "drop-dead gorgeous" and "Bethany Fields" in the same sentence.

But I knew who she was immediately—the one sitting at the booth between Sam's best friend Marko and Sam himself. I couldn't see Sam's face as I froze in the doorway of the bathroom because his back was to me. But Marko was doing everything short of drooling out of the corner of his mouth.

It was easy to see why. Bethany was about a size three with enough thick blonde hair for the four of us and cute little dimples everywhere *but* her thighs.

"Why are you just standing here?" Lindy hissed in my ear. "Aren't you going to show her whose turf she's on?"

I was thinking more of bolting for the door and never looking back, but Lindy gave me a shove that landed me almost in Sam's lap.

"Hi, Kif," Marko said. "Feeling territorial?"

I'd normally have smacked him, but my eyes snagged on Bethany. I would have felt a lot better if she'd borne even the slightest resemblance to the Wicked Witch of the West. But she had sweet eyes.

"Scoot over, Marko," Lindy said, insinuating herself into the booth. She shot me a look that read, "Sit down or I'll rip your lips off."

"Hi," Bethany said. "You must have moved here since I left. I'm Bethany. You're—?"

"*Kiffany*," Lindy told her, as if that should say it all.

But Bethany just smiled as if Lindy had informed her I was Jane Doe. It was only then that I looked at Sam. He was staring into a saltshaker.

"How 'bout those Mets, huh?" Marko said. He was enjoying the heck out of the fact that Sam hadn't bothered to tell Bethany he had another girlfriend, and that *I* was it.

It was pretty obvious he wasn't going to do it now, either. Marko and Lindy fell over each other to be the one to do the job.

Bethany's smile de-shimmered. "Oh," she said.

In spite of myself I felt sorry for her, sitting there staring at Sam, who seemed more interested in sodium content than in her, while everybody else at the table gloated. I wanted to run more than ever, but she caught me with her eyes.

It was definitely strange. They didn't say, "You better be sure you have your hooks in tight, girl, because here I come." I was pretty sure they said, "But I thought he'd be here waiting for me."

I couldn't believe he hadn't been.

The next day was the longest on record. That's the way it is when suddenly you're in unfamiliar territory.

I still thought Sam had the greatest legs God ever put in a pair of soccer shorts, but everything else was different.

I watched every flick of his eyebrow, looking for clues that he still thought I had the clearest skin, the shiniest eyes.

I searched every inch of his face for answers and wondered if it would help if I developed some dimples. Had a hair implant? Went on a diet—a *big* diet?

With all that stuff crammed into my brain, it was hard to look at anything the same way. But the weird thing was, Sam acted like everything was a carbon copy of what it had always been. Even after Bethany had excused herself from our booth with more poise than *I* could have mustered under the circumstances, Sam had looked up from the salt and started talking about soccer and homework—everything but Bethany.

All that day at school while I badgered myself with questions, he smiled his magic smile and got into a fake wrestling match with Marko and acted like nothing in the world was wrong. But to me, that in itself was all wrong. It was driving me crazy.

Sam didn't notice. Marko did.

"Having a bad day, Kif?"

"No," I snapped.

"Oh, so sorry," he said. "I just figured since you were eating your pen cap you might be experiencing a little anxiety."

I looked at my teeth-marked Bic and tossed it across the table.

"Shut up," I said.

"It's getting to you, huh?"

"What?"

"Fields coming back?"

I looked at him blankly. "Who?" I said.

He grinned. "You're scared spitless."

"Shut up," I said.

By the time we got to soccer practice after school, I couldn't stand it anymore.

Coach paired us off for drills, and when Sam and I went down the field passing the ball to each other, I started in.

"Have you seen Bethany today?" I said.

"Saw her in the library fourth period."

The ball came back to me, and I kicked it harder.

"Did you talk?"

"A little."

I kicked it harder.

"Is she back here for good?"

"I didn't ask her."

Harder.

"Has she changed since she left?"

"I don't know."

"Well, find *out!*" I said, and gave the ball a final whack. It caught him right in the nose.

"Honey, you could be hazardous to somebody's health," he said, tossing the ball back. And then he squinted at me. "Kif, are you OK?"

"No," I said, ripping my hand through my unmowed hair. "Did you and Bethany break up before she left?"

"No." He shrugged. "She moved away. Then there was you."

"Oh," I said.

I was losing it. That's what I decided when I got home that night.

Sam hadn't shown a single sign of wanting to go back with Bethany, but I was still sure that any minute I was going to be dumped for that little dimpled blonde who could fit inside a teacup. Why shouldn't I be? She never lathered *her*self up over a game of soccer or combed *her* hair with a lawn mower.

Yep, I decided, as I pulled the peanut butter and brown sugar out of the kitchen cabinet. Sam and I were going to be history if I didn't *do* something. Maybe I should bake *him* cookies.

Kiffany, I thought sternly as I smashed butter into a bowl with a vengeance, why are you feeling so threatened? Come *on*, what's the worst that could happen?

You could lose Sam.

So—would that be the end of the world?

I stopped, measuring cup in midair. It *would* be. Without Sam, the shine would be gone.

Vaguely I heard my mother answering the door, but I still jumped when Lindy breezed in and pulled a fingerful of dough out of the bowl in one big Lindy motion.

"You're baking cookies?" she said. "Are you sick?"

"Desperate."

"Good," she said. She plopped herself on one of our counter stools. "I'm glad you're going to fight for what's yours. Don't let that little beauty contestant take your man."

I looked at Lindy sideways while I churned at the dough. "Do you think he wants to go back with her?"

"I really haven't got a clue, although you'd think so, the way they were before—" She stopped and started over. "All I know is you can't go down without a fight. Y'know the minute you found out she was back, you started to fade."

I stirred harder.

"Sam's really brought you out, Kif. You can't let him go or you'll go back to shoving your hair into a ponytail and stuff."

Something went through me, and I gripped the spoon. Was Lindy right? Was I as good as nothing without Sam? Was he the only thing that could make me shine?

The thought made me sick.

I handed the spoon to Lindy. "Here," I said. "You make the cookies."

I didn't muster enough courage to tell Sam what I was thinking until after the game the next day when we were in a booth alone at Jake's. I'd given Lindy strict instructions not to let anyone bother us. Out of the corner of my eye I could see her standing guard over Marko.

I sighed and moved our glasses around. "I've been thinking," I said. "And Sammie—I think we ought to at least see other people—I mean besides just each other." I looked into my Cherry Coke. I didn't know what I expected to see in Sam's eyes when I looked up. Relief, maybe. Or confusion at the very most. Anger? Nah.

But that's what flashed in them when he lifted my chin with a jerk.

"Why?" he said like his teeth were glued together.

"Well, I just—"

"It's because Bethany came back, isn't it? Man, Kiffany, I've hardly even looked at her! What do you want me to do, have her bumped off?"

"No! It isn't Bethany."

Sam's eyes narrowed, and he leaned back in the booth. "It's another guy."

"What?"

"You like somebody else. You could've just come out and said it."

"It isn't another guy. It's *me*."

Sam shook his head. The magic smile was a million miles away. "I don't get it," he said.

"I'm not sure I do either. I just have to know some stuff—" I would have explained the rest to him if he hadn't lurched out of the booth with his face twitching.

"That's it?" he said.

"I didn't say that was *it*. I just said I thought we ought to see other people."

"It's all or nothing for me, Kiffany," he said. "You made me feel like I was important. I don't want to feel half-important."

I looked back into my crushed ice. "Then I guess that's it," I said in a voice I barely recognized.

And that *was* "it." Sam walked away.

Sadly I watched him slump into a chair beside Marko. Then the door opened, and Bethany came in. She looked around, and like two glasses of Cherry Coke their gazes clinked together. It didn't surprise me that he got up and they sat at a table together.

Lindy slid into my booth, mouth already in motion.

"*What* is going on?" she said.

"We broke up."

"Bethany."

"Sam doesn't care about Bethany."

Lindy shot her eyes toward their table. "You could've fooled me."

"He doesn't care about her as 'Bethany.' I don't think he cared about *me* as Kiffany Cameron. It's the way I made him *feel* and the way she makes him feel and how he made me feel—all shiny."

Lindy was staring at me blankly. "This is a bad thing?"

"Do you remember how we learned in church," I said, "that God makes everybody special? You shouldn't need some other person to *make* you special. I didn't like feeling so threatened because I might lose Sam and not *shine* anymore—and I was right. Sam has to have somebody to shine—and I don't want to be like that."

I was starting to cry. You don't lose your first boyfriend—the one with the great soccer legs and the magic smile and the peanut butter cookies—without at least a few tears.

Lindy was shaking her head. "You tell the guy to take a hike and now you're crying, but you're going to go look for yourself anyway. You've lost me."

"That's OK," I said. "I haven't lost *me*." I snorted out a laugh-cry. "I sure hope that's what counts, because I really want to shine again."

ALWAYS BLONDE ENOUGH

FALL

"He's going to own a BMW before he's twenty-five."

"I bet he eats tofu already."

Hope looked across the cafeteria at Brice Bennett and then back at Lucia and Abby.

"What makes you think he's going to be this yuppie?" she said.

Lucia snorted. "Because he'd only been here about six weeks when he got elected Student Council Vice-President."

"So?"

"*Because*," Abby finished for her, "he knows how to work the cafeteria."

At the moment he wasn't working the room. In fact, Hope noticed, he was sitting by himself at a table, something nobody *dared* do unless they wanted people to think nobody wanted to be with them. And he looked perfectly content to be eating his French bread pizza alone. Wearing his Club Med sweatshirt. Running his hand back over his dark hair. Casually looking over the place with his brooding eyes. Like somebody out of *LA Law*—

"I think he's cute," Hope said.

"Well, dream on," Abby said. "He hasn't even looked at a girl since he moved here."

"That type doesn't look at girls. He waits for girls to look at him." Lucia rolled her eyes. "And then when they do it's like he can hardly make the effort to give them a glance. Gag me one time."

"Yeah," said Abby. "Give me the Sloppies any day."

While Lucia and Abby went off on a discussion of the lineup of freshman boys in their church youth group whom their advisor had dubbed "the Sloppies" because they schlepped around in baggy jeans and T-shirts and only combed their hair on demand, Hope looked at Brice over her milk carton.

Nah, Abby and Lucia were all wrong about him. He didn't strike her as a snob. He was just different from what they were all used to. He wore pants that actually fit and shirts that didn't have writing on them. He got straight A's and didn't say it was because his parents would kill him if he didn't. Even though she hated the whole popularity thing of the Student Council, she admired him for getting himself elected when anybody else would've still had a new-kid stigma surrounding him.

Besides, what was wrong with a guy who didn't fall all over you? Since she'd discovered all boys weren't absurd little creeps, Hope had had plenty of guys like her. But they had always been from among the Sloppies, who tackled her in football and tickled her at church parties and once in awhile held her hand on a bus. A boy she might have to work at a little— now *that* was a challenge.

"I'm going to go talk to him," she said suddenly.

"No way!"

"I am." Hope put her milk carton down and got up. While they muffled shrieks behind her she strolled casually across the cafeteria and slid in beside Brice.

"Hi," she said.

"Hi," he said back.

OK. Now what?

Hope resisted the temptation to glance back at Abby and Lucia and instead leaned over Brice's tray.

"I'm doing a survey," she said. "I just want to find out how new people in the school like cafeteria food—you know, as compared to their old school."

She wasn't sure where that inspiration had come from, but it was better than scurrying back to her friends who were waiting with an I-told-you-so.

"On a grossness scale of one to ten it's up there in the el-stinko category," he said.

"That's what I figured."

"I'm not really all that new anymore," he said.

"Yes, you are. You haven't met me, have you?"

"You aren't in Student Council. That's mostly where I hang out."

"You need to broaden your horizons." Thank heaven for her older sister Meredith, who was always spouting clichés like that. "I think you should come to our church youth group party Friday night."

He glanced over at Abby and Lucia who were by now lean-ing so far off their bench they were holding onto each other to keep from falling to the floor. They both snapped to a minute examination of their fingernails when she looked at them.

She took a deep breath. "You could go with me," she said to Brice.

How was she going to explain that to her parents, who preached "you don't ask boys out" right along with "thou shalt not kill"?

"OK," he said.

"OK what?" she said stupidly.

"Yeah. OK, I'll go with you."

Hope looked triumphantly over her shoulder at the girls and then leaned into Brice's tray again. "Are you going to eat the rest of that?" she said. "I can help put you out of your misery."

"We will make a striking couple," she said to her mirror. "Him with his dark, haunting look. Me with my blonde, sunny one."

"You've been reading too many Victorian novels," Meredith said from the doorway.

"Yeah, yeah, I'm weird," Hope said.

"Weirder than usual." Meredith came into the room and motioned to the four outfits which were strewn across the bed. "I've never seen you be so choosy about what you were wearing—or what your hair looked like. I mean, good grief, I went in to take a shower and you had used half a bottle of conditioner. What gives?"

Hope looked at her cool, together, nineteen-year-old sister in the mirror. Meredith would be able to tell her whether she was crazy or not. She knew about this stuff.

"I'm going to the party with this new guy—Brice Bennett. And Mer, he is *so* fine—"

"And you're a nervous wreck because you want everything to be perfect and you don't want to look like a cutesy teeny-bopper, right?"

"Did you read my journal?" Hope said.

"Come on, I was fourteen once. It's normal to be nervous

and want to be just right for him if it's somebody you're really crazy about. Go for it. Now, I suggest—"

"Hope." Her father tapped lightly on the bedroom door. "Uh, Mr. Bennett is here."

"I've got to check this guy out," Meredith said. "And don't worry—I won't embarrass you."

Meredith dashed out, and Hope's father chuckled. "What's wrong with that kid?"

"Brice?" Hope said. "Nothing."

"Yes, there is. He's fourteen and he dresses better than I do. I almost asked him what his action was like on the stock exchange today."

"Daddy!"

"I didn't. I was cool." He looked at her closely. "You look cute, Honey. Don't change a thing."

That was easy for *him* to say.

In spite of the tiny run in her left sock and the way her hair was too curly on one side, it was a neat evening.

The Sloppies all gave Brice the once-over when he came in and went back to their game of Hacky Sack. Abby and Lucia were in a clump of girls who *all* suddenly had a fetish for their fingernails. But once the food appeared and they got into a game of "Truth or Dare," they lightened up, and so did Hope. After all, this was her turf she was introducing Brice into. And he got into it. He even confessed when it was his turn that he'd been known to write book reports without reading the books. The Sloppies loved that.

They also loved it when Hope owned up to still sleeping with her teddy bear.

Matt Crenshaw howled. "I remember that from the retreat. Man, that thing *smells!*"

Hope tackled him, though, and made him scream uncle before they went on to the next round.

"Did you have fun?" Hope asked when she and Brice were walking home later.

"Weird, freaky people, but yeah."

"Good."

"Only—"

Hope cocked her head at him nervously. "Only what?" *You don't want to go out with me anymore. You think I'm a geek. You—*

"I think you're just a lot more mature than those people let you be, that's all."

Something melted in Hope. "You *do?*" she said.

He slid his hand into hers. "Yeah," he said huskily, "I do."

Don't change a thing? Oh, Daddy, no way. I'm going to change everything.

WINTER

"Hope Fessler, this is an official kidnapping."

"You are coming with us to the mall."

Hope stood up from tying her running shoe and laughed at Lucia and Abby. "I can't, you guys. I've got to jog, and then I need to write a Student Council proposal."

"But first you're going to the mall," Lucia said.

"Because you've gotten totally boring lately," Abby said.

Hope sagged happily. She'd missed these guys the last few months, since Brice. "OK, just for a little while. But let me change. I look like a scuzz-bag."

"You look normal," Lucia said, and grabbed her by the sleeve of her sweats.

"Now," Abby told her when they were standing at the jewelry counter at Penney's, "First we drool over everything, buy a couple things we don't really need—and then we go to McDonald's and split a large order of fries three ways."

"Just like old times," Lucia put in. "Or don't you remember?"

"Of course I remember." Hope grabbed a large pair of earrings shaped like globes. "Hey, guys, how about these?"

"They're you. You gotta have them!"

Hope formed a life-sized picture of what Brice would say if she showed up with the world hanging from her earlobes and put them down.

"I know where I want to go," she said. "Let's look at the hair stuff. I want to get some Sun-In for when the weather gets warmer."

"What's that?" Lucia said.

"You put it in your hair before you go out in the sun and it makes it lighter."

Abby stopped at the foot of the escalator. "Whose idea was that?"

"Brice's," Hope said. Why she felt guilty saying it she didn't know. "Do you have a problem with that?"

Abby shrugged. "I guess not. It's just that—" She looked at Lucia. "You were always blonde enough before."

SPRING

"OK, you've got the registration form in front of you?"

"Yes, Bricey."

"Hope, would you stop calling me that? It's lame."

Hope switched the phone to her other ear and spread out her registration form. "OK, OK. Now—what did you want to talk about?"

"Obviously if we want to be in the same classes next year we've got to take the same courses."

"No kidding?"

"Come on, Hope, get serious. Now—I've got down Algebra II."

Yuck.

"And that chemistry course—"

"That's for juniors."

"You can get into it as a sophomore if you apply for it."

"Why would we want to?" Hope envisioned herself surrounded by lab reports for an entire weekend and shuddered.

"Because then junior year we'll have that slot open for double math courses so we can get calculus senior year."

Hope was quiet. The butterflies that had just about taken up permanent residence in her stomach lately were flapping for attention again.

"What's the matter?" Brice said.

"I don't know—I mean, that isn't what I have down—I mean, for me."

There was a suspicious pause. "What do you have down?" he said.

"Well, I'm really interested in art, you know, and they didn't have any good courses in junior high and now that we're going to Madison—"

"Art? Do you know how far that's *not* going to get you?"

"And since I'm going out for track and girls' basketball and I want to take that after-school course they're offering at church, I kind of didn't want to load myself down with more big academic courses than I needed."

"What about the leadership class?"

Hope squirmed. "What about it?"

"Are you leaving a slot for it in case you get elected to Student Council office?"

"There's no way I'm going to get elected."

"Would you knock it off with the low self-esteem?"

"It isn't low self-esteem," Hope said faintly. "I'm just not running."

There was no pause this time. Brice went for the jugular. "Do you know what a total cop-out that is?"

"It isn't a cop-out. I just—"

"You're just afraid you won't win so you don't want to run. Or if you get elected it might be too much work so—"

"Brice—could we talk about this later?"

"When?"

Hope held the phone away from her ear and glared at it.

"You're copping out, Hope," he said.

Am I? she thought as she went back to her room. Brice had been telling her for so long that she could be so much more sophisticated than she was, get better grades than she did—it was hard now to know which was his voice in her head and which was hers.

But he was the cutest, most popular, most everything guy she'd ever had in her life. He *was* just trying to help her be all that she could be, after all.

"Knock, knock," Meredith said from the doorway.

Hope half-smiled at her and flopped down on her bed.

"Ooh," Meredith said. "Black cloud over tepee."

"You got that right."

"Me help, Kimosabe."

Hope sat up. "Didn't you tell me back when I first liked Brice that I should do everything to be perfect for him?"

Meredith curled her lip. "Did I say that?"

"Yeah. That first night."

Meredith sat down on the bed. "I didn't mean do everything he wants you to do so you'll be his idea of the perfect girlfriend. I just meant if you really like somebody you naturally want to be at *your* best. You know, bring out everything God made you to be."

Hope picked up her teddy bear and rested her chin on his head. "But what if he's asking you to do things to make yourself better?"

"You mean, change things about yourself?"

"Yeah."

Meredith looked uncomfortable. "Is Brice the reason you took a sudden interest in student government and stopped watching *Brady Bunch* reruns?"

"Sort of."

"And started doing this?"

Meredith picked up the Sun-In box and looked at the tanned blonde on the front.

"He just wants me to be—"

"Somebody else!"

"No!"

"Look, Hopey, if somebody tries to help you change something that isn't healthy for you—I mean, like if you were cutting classes all the time and he wanted you to stop—that's OK. But if he wants a whole personality transplant—if he doesn't even like the color of your hair the way it is—he's never going to be satisfied. And besides—that's not fair. If he doesn't like the basic you—"

"Phone for you, Hope!" her father called from downstairs.

Hope trailed drearily out into the hall and picked up the phone.

"Hi, guy!" Lucia said. "I'm filling out my registration form. Are you taking home ec?"

"I have to save a slot for leadership class." Hope said woodenly.

"Why?"

"Because—"

But Lucia didn't let her finish. "Get a clue, Hope. You hate that whole Student Council scene! You're just doing it because of Brice, aren't you?"

Hope hesitated. Her father appeared and pulled his finger across his throat.

"I need the phone," he whispered.

"I'll call you back," Hope said, and hung up.

"Thanks, Honey." Her dad pushed his hand through her curls as he'd been doing since she was in a highchair and then stopped. "What did you do to your hair?" he said.

"You don't like it?"

Her father looked at her for a minute, and Hope looked

back in surprise. There was a sadness in his eyes.

"It's different," he said finally.

Suddenly, Hope had her arms around his neck. "I was always blonde enough before, wasn't I, Daddy?" she said.

"Yeah, Honey," he said softly. "You were."

SUMMER

There was no use pretending she was having a marvelous time, Hope decided as she smoothed on her suntan lotion. Even if she no longer had Brice in her face constantly, it still would've been neat to have him beside her on the beach towel like they'd planned all winter.

"Heads up!" somebody yelled. Hope brought hers down instead and narrowly missed being decapitated by a Frisbee.

"Learn to throw that thing!" she called to Matt Crenshaw.

"Get up off your buns and show me!" he said. "You're not going to turn into one of those chicks that just *sits* on the beach all summer are you?"

"You'll wish I did!" she said and snatched the Frisbee from the sand just as his hand reached for it. "Catch this, fool!"

She hurled the Frisbee toward the waves and then went after it herself. Matt grabbed it the moment she did and both of them came down in a tangle of saltwater and bathing suits.

"Enough!" she said a half-hour later.

"Wimp!" another of the Sloppies said.

Hope ignored him and fell happily onto her beach towel. Lucia and Abby had arrived and were trying to pitch an umbrella.

"Oh, that's disgusting," Lucia said.

Hope followed her gaze and giggled. The Sloppies were standing, mouths at half-mast, gaping at a bronze, bikini-clad person strolling down the beach who obviously had recently stepped off the cover of *Seventeen* magazine.

"Look at them slobber over her," Lucia said.

"Why aren't they slobbering over us?" Abby said.

Lucia poked her with her foot. "Because we can't compete. We aren't thin enough."

"No—we aren't round enough."

"Or wiggly enough."

Hope stood up slowly and snapped her bathing suit into place. "I don't know about you two," she said, "but I can compete."

Lucia snorted. "Yeah. How?"

Hope laughed and took off across the sand toward the Sloppies.

"Because I'm blonde enough!" she called back to them.

Yeah, baby—she thought happily—*God made me blonde enough.*

TECHNICALLY SPEAKING

"Winnie!" Michael called out behind me.

I turned my head toward the beach to smile at him, just in time to see him pointing and yelling something else I couldn't hear over the surf.

"What?" I shouted—and felt my whole body being bowled over. I went head over heels three times and inhaled at least half a gallon of saltwater and sand.

I think he must have said, "Watch out for that breaker."

I landed right at his feet in one crazy slide across the hard sand. I could feel the tiny, crushed-up shells digging into my flesh like a carpet burn. Michael came down beside me with a splash.

"Are you OK?" he said.

"Yeah."

"Klutz. Can you get up?"

"Yeah."

"Want a hand?"

"Want a punch in the mouth?"

We grinned at each other as I sorted out my legs and got to a vertical position. Blood was running down the side of my thigh, and the skin was practically yelping at the invasion of salt into the wound.

"Gross!" I said.

"You better go back to the house and get that cleaned up.

Looks like you lost an inch of skin. Want me to go up with you?"

"Nah." I shook my head. "You'd miss too much tanning time."

"Maybe Terry could go."

I gave him a look. "I'd have to have a fractured skull before I could tear her away from Levi."

"Those two need to be surgically removed from each other."

I grinned and headed up the beach. "I'll catch you later," I said over my shoulder.

"Later," he said.

No chance of you and I ever having to be surgically removed from each other, I thought ruefully as I navigated across the hot sand and started up the path toward the house. But I shrugged that off. I wasn't down here to snag Michael Cannell into romance. The other thirteen people from my church youth group, plus our advisor, and I were here to live it up in the house Michael's uncle had opened up to us for five summer days, have fellowship around the barbecue every night, and improve our snorkeling and body surfing.

I snorted softly to myself as I opened the front door. Good luck on that last one. I was just thankful Terry hadn't seen me take that dive. She'd still be laughing.

And then I *heard* her laugh. Right there in the house. I stopped on the bottom step and listened.

There was no way. Terry was down on the waterfront somewhere, spending as much time snuggling up to Levi in the water as she was swimming. But I heard it again. It was Terry's husky giggle, coming from one of the boys' rooms on the first floor. Then I heard Levi's laugh. There was no mistaking his deep throaty chuckle.

Terry and Levi were in his room together.

What should I do? Burst in on them like the vice squad? Pretend I didn't hear them and hightail it out of there, still oozing blood?

I backed down the steps and listened again. Maybe I was wrong—

But Terry giggled and something smothered it. I lurched for the door, and ran smack into the rack in the entrance hall we used for our towels. The whole thing turned over on the tile floor with a thud. I scrambled up the steps like a cat, and all I heard below was Terry whispering loudly, "Levi, there's somebody here!"

I hid in the bathroom until my blood clotted. When I came out, they were gone.

Everyone commented that night on how quiet I was being. I hoped Michael didn't think I was snubbing him, but he was the least of my worries. Terry was the one I was concerned about. Man, after all our talks about how we were both going to wait for marriage, and I'd practically caught her in the act. On a church trip, no less!

By the fifth time I told someone I was OK, they all stopped asking me and went on cooking hot dogs. But the minute I turned out the light in our room, Terry was on me.

"It was you who knocked over the towel rack this afternoon, wasn't it?" she said.

I came up on one elbow and before I could censor myself I blurted out, "Terry—are you still a virgin?"

There was only a split second of silence before she said

indignantly, "Of *course* I am!"

I didn't say anything. It wasn't that I didn't believe her. It was just that something didn't fit.

She snapped on the light and sat facing me. "Look, Levi and I have—fooled around a lot—"

"You don't have to give me the details—"

"—but we haven't actually, you know, done it—and we don't plan to. Technically speaking, I *am* still a virgin."

"Oh," I said, stupidly.

She sighed in a big-sisterly way. "You can't judge me, Winnie," she said. "When you feel about somebody like I do about Levi, you'll find out how hard it is to just hold hands."

This time I didn't even say "oh." She sighed again and turned off the light.

By the next day at lunch time, I was more exhausted from seesawing back and forth in my mind than I was from mastering the boogie board. Where did Terry get off thinking she was so much wiser than me, just because she was "experienced"? *Did* she know something I didn't when it came to how far you should go with a boy?

I spotted Michael sitting at a table in front of one of the food stands, and he grinned and waved me over. I *did* feel about somebody the way she did about Levi. But would I make the same decision she had if I were given the chance?

"Is your surfing going that bad?" Michael said when I sat down.

"Nah," I said. I unwrapped my corn dog without interest. He dove into his second plate of chicken wings.

"Man, I used to be satisfied with just one order of these," he said as he stuffed one in. "Now I need at least two before I can stop."

I stared at him. "Do you think that's the way people feel about sex?"

"Excuse me?" he said. He choked and snatched up his Pepsi.

"You must need more and more until you're satisfied?" I said.

He looked around uneasily. The party at the next table were all stealing glances at me from behind their soda cups.

"I wouldn't know, Winnie," he said. "Would you?"

"I'm talking about Terry, fool. When I went back to the house yesterday they were in Levi's room. She told me last night that they haven't—you know—"

"Gotcha."

"But that it's OK because they can do a lot of other stuff, and she's still a virgin."

Michael stopped in mid-bite. "Do you think they're up there now?"

"Probably."

He put the wing back on the plate and wiped the grease off his fingers. "I feel like we ought to do something."

"What? Go in there with a warrant?"

He frowned, and then his face lit up. He grabbed the plate of wings with one hand and my arm with the other. "No," he said. "We go in with a plate of wings."

When we came through the kitchen door, Terry was sitting at the counter, and she jumped a foot. She couldn't hide the fact that her next glance was a nervous one past us to the door.

"Looking for Levi?" Michael said.

She glared at me. "Thanks, Winnie," she said, and then she sighed again in that superior way that made my blood curdle. "He's supposed to meet me here. We don't leave the beach together."

"Terry, if this isn't wrong, how come you have to sneak around?" I said.

"Chicken wings, anyone?" Michael said quickly. He plucked one out of the pile and went to work on it. "Here's the deal," he said, mouth full. "I can eat all of these I want, because even once they're gone, I can always order more. But once something like, say, your virginity is gone, that's it—you can't get another one."

Terry gave me a look. "I told you that I'm still a virgin and I'm planning to stay that way." Her eyes narrowed. "I didn't expect you to share all that information with the world."

"So the point is," Michael went on, "it won't be long before you either have to give up Levi or give up being a virgin. In that respect, it *is* like eating chicken wings."

"*What* are you talking about?" Terry's husky voice wound up angrily, but Michael plowed on.

"I can't sit here and look at these things and not eat them, because I love them. Used to be I could be content with a few but now—I gotta have the whole thing."

"So you're telling me that even though I'm not actually having sex with Levi I'm still committing fornication?" She rolled her eyes. "Well, since you two are such experienced lovers—"

Something popped into place inside me. It was the something that hadn't fit last night, but now it did.

"I don't have to be experienced to know it's wrong in God's eyes," I said. "Just like I don't have to steal or murder to know if I do I'm just going to end up hurting myself and somebody else in the end. That's what the commandments are for."

"The way I see it," Michael said, "why tempt yourself?"

He was toying with a chicken wing, but he didn't seem interested in eating it anymore. I studied the countertop, and Terry sat with her arms folded across her chest.

"We ought to get back," Michael said finally.

I looked at Terry. "You coming with us?"

She didn't look back as she shook her head.

"Share these with Levi," Michael said, a little bitterly, I thought. He shoved the plate toward her, and we left.

We ran into Levi on the road. He mumbled something about needing more sunscreen.

"He needs chicken wings," Michael muttered.

That was all either of us said for most of the afternoon, except for that one moment on the beach blanket when Michael turned to me and said, "I don't want you to think I'm judging Levi. I might do the same thing if I were in his place." He looked down at his hands. "That's why I don't get myself into his place."

I stifled a smile. That definitely explained a lot.

But I was still feeling like a piece of cardboard that night when I turned out the light before Terry came into the room. She'd been avoiding me all evening, and I wanted to be asleep before she started sighing at me.

I was still awake, though, when she came in and, to my surprise, sat on the edge of my bed.

"Thanks for caring," she said.

I didn't know what to say, so she went on.

"What you and Michael said really did make sense. I even tried to explain it to Levi." She sighed, but it wasn't at me. "He didn't get it," she said. "We broke up."

I sat straight up in bed and put my arm around her. "I'm sorry," I said. "I know you probably don't believe it, but I am."

"It's OK, really. I thought he was different—I mean, good grief, he seems like such a good Christian—but he isn't, so— that's it, and I'm fine."

She wasn't. I could tell by the stiff sound her voice had. But I knew Terry—she didn't want sympathy. She'd handle it her own way.

"Hey," I said, "did you eat those chicken wings?"

I could feel her grinning in the dark. "No. They're in the fridge."

"Let's go for it," I said.

We polished off most of the plate and contemplated waking up Michael to see if he knew where we could get more.

"Yes!" Terry said, licking her fingers. "Something I can have as much of as I want!"

She beat me to the last one.

I ALREADY HAVE
A MOTHER!

"The movie was awesome!"

"Yeah, Maren, it was."

"The pizza was awesome!"

"Right. Pepperoni is my life."

"The devotion at the end was awesome!"

"Great. I'm sure God appreciates that."

"*I* was awesome!"

"Get the net."

"Jeremy was awesome."

Pammy rolled her eyes. "Oh, brother."

I dropped my canvas bag on her bed. "Come on, Pammy. You have to admit he's the cutest boy in our youth group. In the freshman class. In the—"

"If you say 'on the planet,' these are going right down your throat," she said, threatening me with the pair of pajamas she was holding. "Do you know how disgusting you're getting with this crush on Jeremy?"

But as I flopped down on her bed, she laughed. I did, too. Long and loud.

"It isn't just a crush, Pammy," I said, still guffawing. "I'm in love."

"Get over yourself!"

Of course, I knew as well as she did that what I felt for Jeremy Barrons wasn't love. But he was the first boy I'd ever gotten ripples up and down my esophagus over just because he walked down the hall and said hi to me. And tonight, at our church youth group end-of-the-month party, he'd done more than say hello.

"He sat next to *me* at the movie instead of Bryan," I pointed out. "And they're usually, like, attached at the hip."

"That's true love, all right."

"One Coke—two straws."

"Yep. The genuine article."

"And then at Round Table afterwards—"

"Let me guess, you split every piece of pepperoni."

"Almost—"

"Excuse me while I get sick."

I tossed a pillow at Pammy, who was by now in pajamas and heading for the bathroom to brush her teeth—and floss—and brush her hair a hundred times.

"You're a geek," she said, disappearing into the bathroom.

"Oh, yeah? Then get this. Jeremy invited me to ride my bike down to Davis Park tomorrow afternoon and play Frisbee with him."

Pammy's head reappeared in the doorway. I gloated shamelessly.

"Tomorrow?"

"You got it," I said. I leaned back on her pile of pillows and folded my arms, waiting for a smile to break over her face. After all, I was the first of us to have a glimmer of a boyfriend—a possibility we'd been talking about since sixth grade.

But there was only a pucker that brought her whole forehead into a question mark.

"Tomorrow?" she said again.

"What—are you deaf?"

"What about your English paper?"

"What about it?"

"It's due Monday."

"Yeah. So?"

"Maren, how are you going to go play Frisbee with Jeremy Sunday afternoon when you have a paper due Monday?" She shook her head and went back into the bathroom.

There it was again.

I didn't even answer her, because there it was again. Pammy, my best friend since we were eleven years old, turning parent on me. And it wasn't the first time. In the past two months, I'd found myself ready to tear up phone books every other time we had a conversation.

"Maren, that nail polish looks cheap."

"Maren, if you'd studied more you could've gotten an A on that history test instead of a B+."

"Maren, you don't have to yell. We can all hear you."

And now—"Maren, how are you going to go play Frisbee with Jeremy Sunday afternoon when you have a paper due Monday?"

Where was the phone book?

I sat there, clenching and unclenching the pillow while I listened to her brush and spit. When she came back in, I glared at her.

"What's the matter with you?" she said.

"Oh, nothing. Except that my best friend just poked this huge hole in my bubble!"

"Well, sor-ry," she said. But she sat on the edge of the bed. "It's cool about Jeremy and everything," she said. "But I'm just worried about your grades. They're not as good as they used to be."

I thought about that. OK. True. A minuses and B pluses instead of straight A's.

"You aren't as serious about things anymore. I'm just being your friend."

Her eyes were droopy with worry. She *cared*. Pammy really *cared*.

I sighed. "OK," I said. And then I smiled. "Have you got anything to eat?"

But the urge to rip up the yellow pages returned full force the next day.

"You're wearing your jeans skirt to church?" she said as I pulled same out of my bag.

"Yeah. Why?"

"To *church?*" was her answer.

Later, after Sunday school, when both of us were talking to Jeremy and Bryan on the way into the church, she stopped me on the steps.

"Are we sitting with them?" she hissed in my ear.

"Looks that way!"

"You won't hear a word of the sermon," she said.

I could feel my lips tightening up. "Why do I need to?" I said. "I've been getting one from you all morning."

As soon as I said it, the hurt lit up in her eyes like birthday candle flames and I wanted to have the nearest surgeon remove my tongue. She flounced into the church and plopped herself down in the back row. Even though Jeremy was now five rows up, glancing nonchalantly around like he wasn't looking for me, I sat down next to her.

"I'm sorry," I said. "That was mean of me."

"Yeah," she said. "It was."

When the service was over, I took my time getting out the front door, just in case Jeremy might want to catch up with me. He did.

"Two o'clock, Davis Park?" he said.

The words formed delicious ripples on my esophagus.

"I'll be there," I said.

We exchanged smiles. He took off across the church lawn, and I looked ecstatically at Pammy. But the look on her face didn't just deflate me. It popped me with a bang.

"What?" I said. My hands were twitching for the city directory already.

"You're still going?" she said.

"Yeah!"

"Ma-ren—"

"Pam-my! You know what?"

"What?" she said.

I put my hands on my hips. Even as I was doing it, even as the words formed on my lips, I knew I shouldn't. But, somehow, I just did.

"You really ought to try to find a boyfriend yourself," I said. "Then you can marry him and have your own kids—and stop mothering me!"

I'd have ended up stomping off—if she hadn't beaten me to it. But before she left, I saw the sting in her eyes.

I was still seeing it two hours later as I sat in the garage next to my bike, listlessly popping the bubble wrap I'd pulled out of an empty box. If I didn't leave in the next ten minutes Jeremy was going to think I'd stood him up, and "true love" would be over before it ever started. But I could only sit there and think about the hurt in Pammy's eyes.

That's the state my mother found me in when she walked into the garage with a pile of laundry. One look at me and she dropped it all on top of the washer and joined me. She even picked up a piece of bubble wrap.

"You look like all the icing has just slipped off your cupcakes, Sugar," she said. "What's up?"

That was my mom. She was never pushy. Never nosy. Which was probably why I always cracked open like an egg when she asked me, "What's up?"

"I like a boy," I said, "and he likes me."

"O-K." I could tell she was trying not to smile.

"And I'm happy."

"So far I don't see the problem."

"I'm only getting B pluses and A minuses, but I like school and I'm learning stuff."

"Right. Your father and I are satisfied."

"It doesn't matter to me that I'm not running for class office this year or trying out for cheerleading. I do other stuff and I have time for *me*." I punched hard at a bubble. "What's wrong with me, Mom?"

She really couldn't help it. She laughed out loud. "I'm sorry, Sugar," she said. "I'm not laughing at you—it's just—Sweetie, there's *nothing* wrong with you. You're making good choices."

"Even if I go off and play Frisbee with Jeremy this afternoon and do my English paper tonight?"

"I think so." She looked at me seriously. "Maren, I'm your mother. If I saw you going off on a tangent, I'd tell you. But I think you're doing just fine. Go for it!"

I don't know how much of that I really heard at the time.

Only one phrase stood out: "*I* am your mother."

Pammy cared about me, but she wasn't my mother.

This lady, who liked me just the way I was and could sit and pop bubble wrap with me in the garage, was my mother. She was the only one who could tell me what to do.

Trouble was—ugh—the way I'd handled it with Pammy.

My mom gave me her new tennis shoes to wear and a neat sweatband for my wrist, and I took off for Davis Park on my bike. It was OK, except I still kept thinking about Pammy and the hurt in her eyes.

Maybe that's why instead of heading right for Davis Park, I took a detour and rode past her house. She was outside with her dad, helping him with yardwork. Of course. And she probably had her English paper all done. And she'd probably already set the table for dinner!

I took off for the park before she saw me. Jeremy was there waiting for me with Bryan. When he saw me coming, with my sweatband doing its job big time, he shoved Bryan toward his bike. It gave my esophagus ripples of their own to see him sending his best friend on his way so he could be with me, but before I even got off my bike I was yelling.

"No—Jeremy—wait!"

He stopped in mid-wave.

"Don't get rid of Bryan!" I said.

Bryan grinned out of a face full of freckles. "Gee—thanks."

"No—I have an idea—just—this'll be cool!"

I knew I wasn't making any sense, but Jeremy just kept nodding at me.

"You know my friend—Pam Seiberg?"

Bryan wiggled his eyebrows. He knew her.

"I want to kidnap her—make her play Frisbee with us—

and then I'll buy everybody a yogurt."

"With toppings?" Bryan said.

Jeremy just shrugged and smiled. I think I could have asked him to write my next term paper, clean out my locker, *and* give me one of his kidneys and he'd have done it. Yep, it was true love all right.

When we got to Pammy's she was just wiping her feet before going in the house—naturally. The look on her face when I pulled up with two boys in tow should've been captured on Kodak.

"Come on!" I said.

"What?"

"We're 'napping you!" Bryan was on the front walk behind me. He was already into it.

"What?" she said again.

I grabbed her hand and pulled her down the front steps. "Is that the only word you know? Come on—you're too serious, Pammy."

"Yeah, you need to lighten up," Bryan said, freckles dancing.

Jeremy just shrugged and smiled.

"There's a time to be responsible and there's a time to be fourteen and have fun. Right now it's time to be fourteen and have fun."

By that time I'd gotten her to her garage and out of the boys' earshot.

"And before you say anything, Pammy," I said, "just remember two things."

She hadn't said a word since her last "what." She was just staring at me and wringing her gardening gloves.

"One," I said. "I'm sorry I hurt your feelings. I shouldn't have been so mean."

She nodded.

"And two. Pam—I already *have* a mother."

For a minute she didn't say anything, and I waited, holding my breath. And then slowly, she smiled.

"I get it," she said.

"Good," I said. "Now get your bike. Oh, and Pammy?"

"What?"

"Don't forget to check your tires and bring your lock."

It was a good thing I'm a fast runner, because she threw her gardening gloves at me.

KEEPING SCORE

"Here we go again," I said that Monday afternoon on the way to the gym after school. "I don't see why if we're already on the flag team we have to go through this whole tryout week to get on for next year." I looked down at Mari, who barely came up to my shoulder. "Be glad all you have to do is play the flute."

Mari's already oversized blue eyes swelled even bigger. "Can you see me waving a flag around? I'd put somebody's eye out!"

I stopped at the Coke machine. "You want anything? I'll buy."

Mari shook her head. "If I drank as much Coke as you do, I'd look like the Goodyear blimp." She swept her eyes over the bulky sweater that covered her thighs. "Even without Coke I look like the Goodyear blimp."

"I used to have that problem," I said, popping open the top of a Classic. "You and Lyndel both still have baby fat. You'll grow out of it."

She stuck out her hand. "OK then," she said. "Just one sip."

I handed her the can—and started keeping score.

What Mari doesn't know is that at our first flag practice, I put a pole right into Megan Wojick's armpit. But at least I'm on the team.

Although with these honkin' bones of mine—I feel like André the Giant out there. But at least I'm thinner than Mari—and definitely thinner than Lyndy. Around them I'm Cindy Crawford.

Yeah—I'm OK.

Mari nudged me with the Coke can. "Here comes Lyndy."

I peered down the hall at my other best friend, Lyndy Calahan, who was hiking toward us with an elfish-looking girl who had enough curly red hair for thirty-seven people.

"Who's that with her?" I said.

"She's that new girl in our math class. Didn't you see her in there Friday?"

I remembered now. I'd checked her in with the thought: *Yikes, she's cute. Bubbly. Oh, but when you get close, you can totally tell she has zits. At least I don't have to fork over cash for Clearasil. Yeah, I'm OK.*

"Hi, Mar, Tara!" Lyndy yelled to us. "You guys know Heather?"

"Hi. Yeah, you're in our math class," Mari said.

I just nodded. Zits or no zits, Heather was the kind of girl who reminded me to feel like André the Giant sticking a pole in somebody's armpit.

"I was showing her where the gym is," Lyndy said. "She's trying out for flag team."

Heather cocked her mane-covered head at Lyndy in surprise. "Aren't you?"

Lyndy snorted. "Right! I guess I could waddle out on the field with a flag in my hand!"

Heather wrinkled her nose. "You have a cute shape! What's the deal?"

Aha! I thought as I began to calculate. *Cute—but insincere. At least I don't out-and-out lie to my friends.*

"I've got to go if I'm going to get there before Mrs. Greenwood starts her little spiel," I said. "Like I don't already know every word she's gonna say."

"Great. You can tell me," Heather said—and she actually fell into step beside me. She flipped her hair around to call out to Lyndy, "I'll call you when I'm done. I definitely want you to show me the mall."

Lyndy will hate that, I registered on my tab. *She hates pushy people. At least* I—

But we'd arrived at the gym and Heather was following me up the bleachers, bubbling away.

"Why doesn't Lyndy try out, anyway? She's got a lot of energy."

"I guess she never thought about it," I said.

Heather wrinkled her nose at me. "That's weird—I mean with you two being so close and all. I'd have thought she'd want to."

The microphone squealed, and Mrs. Greenwood cleared her throat over it—so I didn't have to answer.

Heather drifted off after Mrs. Greenwood's I-don't-care-how-good-you-are-attitude-is-everything lecture, and I took a look at my inner tally. *No, I never suggested to Lyndy that she try out for flag team, but at least* I *didn't invite her to go out there and make a fool of herself.* I decided I didn't owe Heather an explanation anyway. As soon as she found the cool crowd, she probably wouldn't even cock her little head at any of us anymore, much less ask us to take her to the mall. She and Lyndel at the mall together—right.

Tuesday morning, Lyndy and Mari were already at the planter when I got to school. We'd started hanging out at the planter in front of the main office at the beginning of the year because—well, because coming from a Christian school instead of the public middle school, we didn't know anybody. *We may be outsiders,* I'd calculated that first week, *but at least we have a place to be and somebody to be there with.* In fact, that may have been the day when I started keeping score in my head—comparing my worth to everybody else's. As long as I could stay one point ahead, I was OK.

"Check it out—check it *out!*" Mari squealed when I reached them.

Without waiting for me to ask what it was I was supposed to check out, Mari whipped Lyndy's hair back over her ears and squealed again. A tiny gold ball twinkled from each of Lyndy's earlobes.

"You pierced your ears?" I said—stupidly.

Lyndy nodded and beamed. "Last night. My mom and I took Heather to the mall and she talked us both into it."

"Can you stand it?" Mari obviously couldn't because she was dancing around like she had to go to the bathroom.

"I never knew you even wanted pierced ears," I said.

"I always did—but I just didn't think I'd look that good in earrings."

"You do, though," Mari said. "How long before you get to change to some cool ones?"

"A couple weeks—Heather bought me the raddest pair—kind of a present because I've been showing her around and stuff."

"At least I don't try to buy people's friendship."

Their faces looked like they'd been hit with a stun gun. That's when I realized I'd said it out loud.

All the happy shimmer slid from Lyndy's face. "Do you think that's what Heather's doing?" she said.

"No way!" Mari said—and then she shot a wary glance at me. "I mean—Tara—you don't think—"

I wanted to cry, *No! I didn't mean to say that. I only meant to think it!*

But I shrugged and said, "Probably not on purpose. I just don't want you to be disappointed."

There was a funky silence—in which Lyndy's eyes that had been all shiny and excited minutes before filled with tears and Mari fumbled around for something to say. "Did it hurt?" she blurted out. "I mean—when they pierced your ears?"

At least I'd never build you up and then let you down, I entered on my mental program. But it didn't make me feel OK.

Still, I wasn't expecting what happened that afternoon at tryout camp. I was tying my tennis shoe when I heard a familiar voice above me say, "Hi, Tara." I looked up to see Lyndy standing there, smiling again, with Heather at her elbow. Both of them were in PE clothes and ponytails.

"Are you gonna watch?" I said to her. "Cool."

"No!" she said. "I'm trying out!"

Before I could answer, Heather bounced her red clog of curls and said, "Why shouldn't she? You and I can help her."

I stared from one of them to the other. It felt like something was sliding away inside me and I couldn't get hold of it.

"Lyndel," I said, "you've never done this before."

Lyndy looked uncertainly at Heather before she answered. "Neither had you before you tried out."

"Yeah, but—"

"But what?"

I looked at Heather. She was narrowing her eyes at me, like a district attorney you see on TV.

"But what?" she said again. "She isn't an idiot. She has good rhythm and a great smile—and she definitely has the attitude. I'd rather work with her than just about anybody else in this room."

Whatever it was that was sliding away in me made its final break and I was out there—floundering. That's the only way I can explain the fact that I said—I actually *said*—"Yeah, but what about those hips?"

Lyndy's face pinched beneath her ponytail. "What *about* my hips, Tara? You never said anything about that before."

"I don't mean to be mean or anything," I said. "But how are you going to wear a satin jumpsuit? They don't exactly look good on everybody."

"And I don't mean to butt in or anything," Heather said sharply, hands on her hips, "but I think you *do* mean to be mean. I can't believe you said that to your supposedly best friend. Aren't you guys, like, Christians or something?"

"All right, girls," Mrs. Greenwood squealed into the microphone. "Let's spread out for the warm-up."

Heather gave me one last long look, and then she and Lyndy spread out as far away as they could get from me. But I watched them for the rest of the afternoon, and my mind was working like a CD-ROM.

Yeah, Heather's real supportive—but at least I don't give people false hopes.

Yeah, Heather's doing the whole positive attitude thing—but at least I concentrate on my work instead of showing everybody what a team player I am.

Yeah, I'm OK.

But even though I came out ahead on the ledger, I felt worse than ever. I kept thinking about what Heather had said. *Aren't you guys, like, Christians or something?*

Final tryouts were on Friday. By then Lyndy was barely speaking to me and Mari looked like a rubber band being pulled in two different directions. I got to her first to ask her to come see me in the finals.

"I need somebody's support," I told her. "Lyndel's got her own little rah-rah section—of one."

"I'll come yell for you," Mari said. And then her eyes got big as Frisbees. I knew she wanted to add, "But I'm going to cheer for Lyndy, too."

I registered a feeble: *At least I'm not two-faced. I must be OK.*

The gym was teeming with dry-mouthed, sweaty-palmed girls who thought they'd probably die if they didn't make the flag team. I was one of them. And as I sat about six rows up in the bleachers with Mari, I saw Lyndy come in with Heather. She'd actually curled her hair before she put it up and she looked—OK—pretty. I flipped toward Mari.

"You know what I really admire about you?" I said.

She shook her head slowly.

"At least you *know* you can't do this, and you aren't out there making a spectacle of yourself."

Mari didn't answer. She just studied the palms of her hands.

"Tara?"

I looked around. Lyndy was two rows down, climbing over people to get to me.

"I just wanted to wish you good luck," she said as she stood beside me. "Really—I mean it. Not that you'll need it, of course—"

"So—Heather says she thinks you'll make it?" I said.

Words died on her lips, and she looked at me with her mouth still open. It seemed like a long time before she answered. There were no tears in her eyes as she gave her pony-tail a little toss.

"I don't need Heather to tell me I can make it," she said. "I've worked hard this week—I found out I could do things I never dreamed I'd be able to. And you know why?"

"Because Heather—"

But I stopped because she'd put her hand on my arm. "Because all this time, I've been looking *down* on myself. Being around Heather has made me start looking *up* at myself." Her eyebrows went up, like she'd just thought of something. "I guess you look at yourself the way the people closest to you think of you."

With that new thought still tingling on her face, she got up and left.

"Group one!" Mrs. Greenwood called into the squealing microphone. "You're up first. Let's go!"

Mari had to poke me and tell me that was my group. I was so numb I didn't hear it.

I was also so numb I couldn't remember the routine. I blew the tryout.

I didn't even have to look at the list they posted later that afternoon to know that I didn't make the flag team. I was try-ing to just march past it like I didn't care when Mari came belt-ing out of the crowd around the bulletin board and grabbed my arm.

"Tara!" she said. "Lyndy made it! She made it!"

I glared down at her, and she shrank back. "Oh. Didn't you?"

"No," I said. I could feel the tears coming into my voice, but I shoved them down. "But it's no big deal. At least *I*—"

But Mari was already backing away—and looking at me like she was seeing something she'd never seen before.

"I'm going to go catch up with her and Heather," she said. As she walked away, I saw her look down thoughtfully at her thighs, like maybe they weren't so chubby after all. I shook my head clear and tried to start a new column in my head.

But I couldn't think of anything to put in it. There wasn't anybody left to look down on. In fact, the only things left in my head were Heather's words: *Aren't you guys, like, Christians or something?*

What was it I did that she didn't think was Christian? Was it the same thing that had left me standing here—way-far ahead on the score sheet—but without a friend within a six hundred-mile radius?

The tears climbed up the back of my throat again. Maybe that, I decided, was what I ought to start keeping track of.

I WANNA LOSE
~~10~~ ~~20~~ 30 POUNDS

1. *Clean room.*

That had to be number one, but only because my mom had said I couldn't do anything else until she had all the dishes back in the kitchen—I like an occasional snack in my room—and she could see the floor again—I usually change my clothes four times before I decide what to wear, and the rejects seldom find their way back to the closet.

Smiling smugly at the smooth expanse of mauve carpet, I crossed number one off the list and moved on to item two.

2. Call Tif—see what we're doing tonight.

I put a squiggly mark next to that one, the official symbol for "started but not completed."

It had been weird, actually, calling Tif. We always did something on Saturday night. We'd devoured a lot of popcorn and movies together in each other's living rooms since the beginning of middle school. This morning when I'd called Tif, though, she'd said she was going to a party being given by some kids on the district church youth council. Tif was one of the freshman representatives.

"I'll call Brannon and see if it'd be OK for you to come, too," she'd said.

So that item was on hold. I moved to number three.

3. Look for a totally cool career.

Hungrily I grabbed for the stack of Christian college catalogs I'd borrowed from our church library. The fact that I was only in the ninth grade didn't deter me from looking into the future, probably because the present was, frankly, pretty dull.

I popped open a Coke and dug into the sour cream and onion chips as I located the page I'd already marked. Yep, that was going to be me, English professor at a noted Christian college, lecturing on C.S. Lewis, dressed in smashing suits and—

I stuffed in another mouthful of chips, grabbed for the pen, and added—

4. Cut out pictures of possible wardrobe for totally cool career.

I pawed through the magazines in the basket by my bed and found a copy of *Working Woman* I'd acquired from somewhere. My clothes-loving eyes perused the pages of Evan Picone suits and silk blouses.

Everything went just above the knee to reveal the beginnings of slender thighs. I wiped my salty hands on my jeans and wrote—

5. Lose ten pounds.

I checked out my own thighs and edited:

5. Lose twenty pounds.

I flipped a few pages and magically the article title read, "Fashions That Slenderize."

I snatched up the list.

5. Lose five pounds.

6. Locate fashions that slenderize.

Oh, and—

7. Spend quiet time with God.

When my mother had found one of my early lists a few years ago, with entries like "Wash all of Barbie's clothes," she'd taught me always to add that last one and the rest would go better.

"Kelsey! Phone for you!" Mom called from downstairs.

It was Tif. I took it in the kitchen and made a sandwich while we talked.

"Brannon says you can come," she said.

"What are you going to wear?" I said.

She laughed. "I knew you were going to ask that!"

I went through my usual three outfits getting dressed and after my favorite pair of jeans wouldn't zip, I changed number five to *Lose eight pounds.*

There were eleven or twelve other people at the party besides Tif and me, most of them juniors and seniors.

"Kelse, glad you could make it," Brannon said as he took my jacket.

A tall slender girl with Cindy Crawford hair who looked like she never ate anything said, "The food's that way—help yourselves."

"That's Gretchen," Tif whispered to me en route to the dining room.

But my eyes were glued to the table. The only thing missing was caviar.

There was no place to sit in the living room by the time I'd filled my plate except next to Gretchen. She was talking about her recent skiing trip where she'd finally tried a double-diamond slope.

"What are you going to do now that ski season's over?" someone said.

"With the ice off the sidewalks, I can rollerblade!"

The whole conversation made me tired. I turned to Tif, but she was telling Brannon about the play she'd just gotten cast in at school.

"Tif's a good actor," I said.

"Are you in it?" Brannon said.

"Me?" I said. "No—I—don't do theater."

"Oh," he said. He didn't look surprised. "So Tif's into drama and track. What's your thing?"

There was a silence in the room as if they'd all been waiting to hear. My mind flipped back over the day's list.

"Well," I said finally, "I just kind of hang out—I read a lot. Actually, I'm thinking of becoming a college professor."

"This year?" somebody said.

They all laughed. Someone else said, "That's cool," and then the talk turned abruptly to how soon it was going to be warm enough to go to the lake. I smeared out the image of me in a bathing suit and concentrated on the last wiener bagel.

The party had been going about an hour when I finally figured out I had nothing to contribute to the conversation. It was more out of boredom than anything else that I excused myself to the restroom. Brannon's house had one of those neat bathrooms where the toilet is in a separate room from the sink. I had just flushed when I heard Gretchen and another girl talking in the outer room.

"Who's that freshman girl—what's her name?"

"Kelsey," Gretchen said. "She's a friend of Tif's."

"Why? Tiffy seems like she's got a lot going for her. That Kelsey chick is lifeless."

"That's not totally true," Gretchen said. "Kelsey has a really cute face, and she—"

"Yeah, but she could stand to lose about thirty pounds."

"Julia!"

"I know it's mean, but it's the truth."

I heard a voice from down the hall.

"We're coming," Gretchen said, and the bathroom was silent.

I sank down on the edge of the bathtub. As I stared down at my chubby hands, "lifeless" was definitely the word.

I called my mom to pick me up and told Tif I wasn't feeling well, which was the truth. I'd never felt worse in my life.

As soon as I got up to my room, I fumbled for a piece of paper and a pencil and scribbled out a new list.

1. Lose thirty pounds.

I scratched that out.

1. Lose forty pounds.
2. Go roller-skating.
3. Take tennis lessons.
4. Run for student body office.

A tear splashed onto the paper and felt-tip ink dribbled down the page. Sobbing, I drew hard angry lines through everything but number one.

The past year of my life had been pretty boring, but the next two weeks I came alive—with pain. Every minute I was awake, which was most of them, I was miserable.

I used my savings of allowance and baby-sitting money to buy some powdered diet stuff and skim milk for breakfast and lunch, which with some sneaking around I managed to keep a secret. At dinner time I pushed the food around on my plate and ate as little as I could get away with.

That doesn't mean I wasn't hungry. I thought about food constantly. But whenever I'd find myself heading for the kitchen for a package of Oreos, I'd hear those awful words again: "That Kelsey chick is lifeless. She could stand to lose about thirty pounds." Nothing in my life was going to work if I didn't get thin. So I struggled and I starved.

And by the end of the second week, I'd lost five pounds.

It was disappointing to look at the scales and see the needle only go down that far. *You shouldn't be surprised*, I told myself as I looked in the mirror. As far as I was concerned, it still showed a blubbery blob with water beds for hips.

I decided to try another weight loss plan, and I was headed toward the diet store in the mall when my eye caught a display of spring outfits at Nicole's Boutique. It was the first time anything besides a hot fudge sundae had appealed to my mind in two weeks, and I stopped to look.

Wistfully I fingered a long, flowing silk skirt. It was a five—but I'd get into it. Before the end of the summer, I'd get into it.

"Can I help you find your size?" a voice said beside me.

My head jerked up. It was Gretchen. We both said, "Oh," at the same time.

"I *know* this isn't my size," I said. "I was just—"

"It's Kelsey, isn't it?" she said. "Do you remember me from Brannon's party?"

You better believe I remember, I wanted to say. But I just nodded and said, "Why *don't* you show me the size *sixteens?*"

Gretchen put her hand on my arm. "Look—I'm going on break. Can I buy you a Coke or something?"

My stomach churned. "I guess so," I said.

Sitting at a table in the food court, I sipped at a cup of water. I would have drooled over the frozen yogurt she was having, but the lump in my throat wouldn't have let me swallow it.

"When I said that in the store," Gretchen said finally, "I wasn't trying to imply that you couldn't possibly squeeze into a size five. In fact, I was noticing that you've lost weight since the party."

"A little," I said.

"Not that that's the most important thing—"

"It seemed like the most important thing that night!" I blurted out.

"What?"

"When you and what's her name—Julia—were talking in the bathroom. She said I could stand to lose thirty pounds. I've only lost five. Sue me."

I took a slug of water and kept blinking. Gretchen put her spoon down.

"OK, can I defend myself here?" she said.

I shrugged.

"It doesn't matter that *I* said you had a cute face and *Julia* was the one who made the comment about the weight—I was still part of the conversation and we *were* talking about you behind your back and that's totally unchristian. I apologize."

I shrugged again.

"But I hate to see you missing out because you're too tired and lethargic to enjoy your life. I mean, you're talking about stuff you want to do out of *graduate* school, when everything right now is passing you by because—"

"I'm too fat."

"It's not about how you look. It's the way you feel. God wants you to take care of the body he gave you so you can do what he put you here for."

"I'm taking care of it now," I said.

She looked at me suspiciously. "How?"

"Diet."

"Pills?"

"No! It's a powder, skim milk thing. It's safe."

"It won't kill you, if that's what you mean," Gretchen said. "At least—not if you only use it for two weeks."

"I'm changing today."

"To what? Let me guess—another 'safe' thing out of a can."

"Well—"

"You have the look. Your eyes are dull, like you're exhausted—"

"What am I supposed to do? First you people say I'm Jabba the Hutt, so I go on a diet and now I look like a bag lady!"

Gretchen tried not to laugh, but she sprayed happy bubbles of saliva all over the table.

"Just listen to me!" she said. "If you really want to lose weight, for the right reasons, so you'll feel good and you can do fun things and all of that, then do it right."

"Which is how?"

"Eat three no-sugar, low-fat meals a day and get a lot of exercise. And—" she patted my arm, "—don't aim for size five. Little dwarf people wear size five. You and I have bigger bones.

I wear an eight myself. Just find the best *you* and go for that."
She gave my arm another squeeze. "Tif told me you're a
Christian so you probably already know this, but putting God
first helps whenever you're trying to change for the better."

"Is that why you can eat frozen yogurt and still look like
that?" I said longingly.

"It's nonfat and sugar-free," she said, tossing the container
in the trash. "I have to go back to work. My last name's
Karamanoogian. We're the only one in the phone book. Call
me if you want to talk some more, OK?"

As I watched her size eight disappear down the mall, the
words that had been haunting me for a week, "She could stand
to lose thirty pounds," faded a little. In fact, I could hear other
words coming in louder—ones my mom had tried to tell me a
long time ago: "Putting God first helps, really."

I dug in my purse for a pen and pulled a napkin from the
dispenser.

Today, I wrote.

1. Spend thirty minutes with God.
2. Avoid sweets and fat.
3. Walk six times around the mall.

My stomach growled loudly. I went for the bottom of my
purse again and then headed for the counter.

"I'll have a grapefruit juice on ice," I said to the girl in the
apron, "and—do pretzels have any fat?"

Thanks, God, I thought as she tossed a small bag across the
counter.

And then I walked and munched—and started to smile.

THE CLOSED CLUB

I thought everything about Jessica LaMore was sharp. Her eyes. Her fingernails.

Her tongue.

Like that day in class when I was giving her and Kristi Wallen directions to my house for the meeting to work on our English project.

"So, Jill, I suppose you have, like, this perfect house," she said to me.

"I like it," I said.

"No, I mean, I bet the socks are lined up in the drawers in matched pairs and your parents never fight and you say grace at the table every night."

Actually, that was an exact description of my house, but I just shrugged.

Danielle cowered behind her literature book. She'd been terrified of Jessica ever since Mrs. Bertice had put us all in a group together.

Erica leaned forward, and I knew she was going to ask Jessica a question. She was fascinated by her.

"What's *your* house like?" Erica said.

Jessica wiggled her eyebrows. "I don't want to shock you, but my parents are divorced. My brother Rodney has a tattoo. And—" she lowered her voice conspiratorially, and Erica leaned in further. "We never make the beds."

Erica's forehead pulled into a puzzle. Jessica snorted.

"What time Saturday?" said Kristi.

We all stopped and looked at her—because basically she never uttered a syllable.

"Eleven," I said. "My mom said she'd do pizza for us."

Jessica sniffed. "Homemade, of course."

We made an out-of-joint group, the five of us. I know we'd never have ended up doing an English project together if Mrs. Bertice hadn't assigned the teams and said her word was final.

There was snake-tongued Jessica, who made straight A's but lived on the edge with all her teachers.

And silent little Kristi, whose grades and everything else were a secret to us all.

And Erica, Danielle, and me. It was hard to tell which of us was which from the outside, I'm sure. We were all Christians, heavily involved in our church and youth group. We all lived with our original parents and had great families—and we all knew it was God's hand that assured that for us. We had cool lives.

But we were scared spitless.

After eight years of Christian school, venturing into a public high school freshman year was like foraging into the jungle. That's why all of us from church had decided to stick together. We had our own table in the cafeteria and our own parties on the weekends, and whenever we had classes together we stuck to each other like strips of Velcro.

Nobody bothered us—until Mrs. Bertice stuck us with Jessica.

"Do you think she's going to sit here and criticize how clean your mother keeps the floors?" Danielle said Saturday when we were setting up my family room and waiting for Jessica and Kristi to arrive.

"I'm not going to give her a chance," Erica said. "I want to find out about her brother's tattoo. How do they do those?"

"Would you give it up?" I said testily.

"Boy—when it comes to Jessica, you sure get crabby." Erica sniffed.

That was the absolute truth. I didn't like most of the stuff that came out of Jessica's mouth, but I found myself admiring her for some reason. I wasn't sure it was right for me to feel that way, and when I'm not sure of myself, I get cranky.

Jessica arrived her usual five minutes late and appraised my home with one glance.

"Just like I thought," she said. "Perfect."

"Coke or 7-UP?" I said.

She opted for 7-UP and curled up on the love seat where she could see out to the driveway. "Where's Jabber Jaws?" she said.

Erica giggled. "Who?"

"What's her name—Kristi. Don't tell me you three haven't noticed she never speaks more than about five words at a time."

"That's not so bad," Danielle said timidly, and added, "Is it?"

Jessica raised her 7-UP defensively. "I wasn't passing a judgment. Just wondered if you'd caught it. Aren't you curious about why she's so withdrawn?"

Erica's eyes got that "No—tell us!" sparkle. "What do you think?" she said.

I plopped the pizza boxes impatiently on the coffee table. "She's probably just shy."

"No." Jessica helped herself to a large slice of pepperoni with extra cheese and talked on with her mouth full. Danielle nervously slid a napkin across the table toward her. "Shy is when you blush when you laugh and would rather have your braces tightened than give an oral report. This chick never meets your eyes. She cringes when you ask her how she's doing. I mean—Danielle—*you* are skittish, but she makes you look like—I don't know—Roseanne or somebody. There's something going on with her." She licked a string of cheese off her finger and looked around at us. "Oh—" she said. "Were we supposed to say grace first?"

Erica chortled. Danielle retreated to the window. I said quickly, "No—that's OK."

"This must be Kristi's car," Danielle said.

Something about the way Kristi got out of the front seat of the Suburban made me stop en route to the kitchen to watch. Jessica, Erica, and Danielle all froze at the window, too.

Maybe it was the slamming of her car door. Or the flinging open of the one on the driver's side. Or the way the tall, red-faced man emerged and actually doubled his hand into a fist as he screamed at Kristi.

Screamed at her. We could hear the tone of his voice even through the glass. Out of the tirade he was obviously spewing at her, three or four words I'd heard only a few times in my life splattered against the windowpane like the ugly pieces of filth they were. I couldn't move. I could only stare in disbelief that a human being could be that ugly from the inside out.

The scene went on for what seemed like an eternity. Then the man lunged into the car and squealed off down my street before he even got the door closed behind him. A ripple of awkwardness went through the three of us.

Jessica sprang off the love seat and went for the door, tossing her pizza crust onto the coffee table. "The poor kid is sobbing," she said.

Erica followed and peeked from behind the open door, while Danielle picked up the pizza crust and fled to the kitchen with it. I just stood there.

Kristi *was* crying, huskily and in painful-sounding chokes, as Jessica guided her up the walk and into the house. Jessica had her arm around her shoulder, and she got her to the love seat in two strides.

"It's OK, girl, just try to take deep breaths," Jessica kept saying to her. To Erica she said sharply, "Get her some water."

It took a surprisingly short time for Jessica to calm Kristi down. Then she sat there with her arm around her and coaxed her to talk.

"Was that your father?" Jessica said.

"Yeah."

"Does he hit you?"

"No. He just screams."

"No kidding!"

Kristi smiled a little, and Jessica smiled with her.

"How can they laugh?" Danielle whispered to me.

"Hey, look," Jessica said to Kristi, "don't be embarrassed that that happened in front of everybody, OK? If you need to cry, cry. If you need to talk about it, go for it. I'll listen." She laughed ruefully. "I've probably heard it before anyway."

As the three of us stood there, *behind* my family room couch, mind you, Kristi did open up. She spilled out a story about her stepmother and the constant vicious battles in her house that I couldn't identify with even in my wildest imaginings. Through it all, Jessica kept nodding and rubbing Kristi's back until by the time she was through, Kristi's eyes were dry and her hands had stopped shaking.

"I feel better," she said.

"Talking doesn't really change anything," Jessica said, "but at least you don't have to walk around with it inside you, ready to pop like a zit."

There was a silence more uncomfortable than a stone in your sandal. It felt like somebody—like me—should say something.

"Want a Coke, Kristi?" I said.

"No." She stood up shakily. "If you guys don't mind, I really don't feel like working on an English project today. I'll walk home—my dad won't be there."

"I think I'll go home, too," Danielle said. She had her backpack on and was to the end of the driveway, a reluctant Erica in tow, almost before Kristi could get out the door.

From the window, Jessica watched them all go. She shook her head and snorted.

"That really freaked those two out," she said. "I bet they've never seen anything like that before."

"I haven't either!" I said.

She flopped down on the love seat and picked up another slice of pizza. "You guys are lucky," she said. "I guess it's because you all come from churchy families."

"*Christian* families," I said stiffly.

"Look—would you sit down? You make me feel weird, standing there like you're going to make a break for it any second."

I sat down on the couch. My head was spinning.

"I don't know about the Christianity thing," she said. She took another bite and surveyed me while she chewed. "It looks like it works for you people. I mean, you don't cuss, you apparently don't have screaming matches with your parents in the street. But I don't like the idea of belonging to some closed club."

I could feel my mouth falling open. "Closed club?"

"Yeah. You guys move around like you have a fence around you—like you don't want anybody to know the secret that makes your lives so wonderful."

"We don't do that!"

"Sorry, Jill," she said, stabbing the crust toward me in the air. "But you do. You shut the rest of the world out like it's unclean."

"That isn't fair!" I said.

"OK—if Danielle had come in here crying, you and Erica would have been all over her, comforting her. But Kristi—she's not in the club, she's outside the circle—so you stand there and stare at her like you're clueless."

"I *was* clueless! I never knew anybody whose father would go off on them like that."

"What difference does it make what she was upset about?" I opened my mouth to answer her, but nothing would come out. The truth was, it shouldn't have made a difference—and Jessica knew it.

"Well?" she said. She drummed her long, sharp nails on the coffee table and pointed her eyes at me. It made the hair on the back of my neck stand up.

"What?" I said.

"Just for once I'd like to hear what you really think. I mean, you're one of God's chosen, so you must think something."

"I hate that!" I said.

"Ah—she's going to tell me what she thinks."

"I hate it when you make sarcastic remarks about Christianity. You make fun of us because we pray before we eat and don't have abusive fathers. I hate that."

Jessica cocked a quizzical eyebrow. "Then why don't you ever call me on it?"

I looked at her stupidly. "I—don't know."

"I've only studied Christianity from a purely intellectual point of view—I did a report on it in World History—but I thought the whole idea was that you were supposed to be out telling the whole story about Christ to us nonbelievers. Frankly—" she flung a leg over the arm of the love seat "—I think you're a bunch of snobs who think the rest of us aren't good enough for you."

It was a strange moment to discover it, but as I sat there with her words stinging my face, I figured out what it was I admired about Jessica. She wasn't afraid to say what she believed. And my little knot of Christians—we were.

It was obvious it was time I stopped being scared, because she wasn't going to leave until I did.

Self-consciously I flung *my* leg over the arm of the couch and picked up a piece of now cold pizza. "OK—I'll share something with you," I said. "You were wrong when you said nothing could really change for Kristi and her father. Christ could help them, and I know how they can get to him."

Jessica made her eyes go big. "Ooh—but are you going to tell?—that's the question."

I pointed the pepperoni with extra cheese at her. "I'd appreciate it if you wouldn't make fun of me or my faith," I said.

For a minute sharp, sarcastic eyes met Christian ones, and for a minute I had a flash of what it must have been like for Jesus, looking into the faces of people outside his circle. Jessica sat back on the love seat.

"OK," she said. "Tell me how Jesus could solve Kristi's problems."

I did tell her. It was scary. I'd have to tell Danielle that. And Jessica's questions were fascinating. I'd have to tell Erica that. But I wasn't confused anymore.

The first chance I got, I was going to tell Kristi that.

FREAKING OUT

NEWS
FLASH

OVER THE FUTURE

THE GENNY GENE

"Cool—another noble American citizen makes an ethical decision that changes the face of integrity forever."

Jonathon switched off the TV and stretched. "And on a Friday afternoon rerun of *Matlock*."

I ignored him, because, after all, he's my seventeen-year-old brother and I always ignore him. But I was thinking basically the same thing, only without the sarcasm.

"Genevieve—telephone!" my mother shouted down from upstairs.

"You ought to just attach one to your ear permanently," Jonathon said drily as he headed for his room.

I ignored that, too, and scrambled up the stairs for the extension phone in the hall. My mind was still on ethical decisions when I picked up the receiver.

"It's Rache," said the perky voice on the other end.

"I'm glad you called," I said. "I'm freaking out."

"Over what?" Her voiced warmed to it. She loved to pull me out of my little pits of despair.

"I don't know how I'm going to make all these decisions that are ahead. What if I really mess up and end up being a shoplifter or something?"

"*What* are you talking about?"

"I'm talking about the reporter on *Matlock* who was locked up because he wouldn't reveal his source. We're, like, maturing now, Rache. We've got to start thinking about stuff like that."

There was a blank in the phone line for a minute, and then Rachel snorted. "All I'm thinking about is that Marty wants us to go out tonight to get pizza. His parents are letting him use their pickup."

"We've got First Amendment rights to worry about—and maybe even Fifth—"

"Do you want to go or not?" Rachel said.

I sighed. Obviously Rachel was going to be no help. "Sure—what time?"

I think she said seven. I was already back to *Matlock* by that time.

OK—I know it sounds bizarre, but seeing that show started some kind of mechanism going in my brain. My dad calls it the Genny gene—this thing that starts when I get an idea in my head. All I could think about right now was, how *was* I going to make all the tough choices that were obviously waiting out there to eat me up like big sets of alligator teeth?

I made a dive for Jonathon's door.

"Hey, Jonathon!" I said through the crack. "You got any spare notebooks?"

Jonathon always had extra empty notebooks, not to mention sharpened pencils with actual erasers. He was this *student* who always knew where everything was.

He stuck a blue spiral notebook out the crack and leaned on the door to watch me take the steps three at a time. "What are you doing?" he said.

"Survey," I said.

I headed for the kitchen, where most of my best information comes from in one form or another, and my dad had just come home from work. He, too, was taking a survey—of the refrigerator.

"Dad," I said, flopping down on a counter stool and wrapping my legs three times around it. "How do you make really tough decisons—the ones that involve ethics?"

"Hi, Genny. How was your day?" he said. He pulled out a jar of salsa and gave me his here-we-go-again look.

"Dad, I'm serious. How do you—"

Dad put his hand up, which means "Genny, hush up and give me seven seconds to answer you." I gnawed my pencil.

"Genny-girl," he said, "what I do is I don't borrow trouble. Your worst problem right now ought to be what to do with that hairdo."

I clutched at my wild mop of tresses, which I currently had tied into a ponytail on top of my head with a scrunchie.

"Be a kid while you can," he said, and then stuck his head into one of the cabinets. "Did your mother buy any more chips?"

As if on cue, Mom suddenly yelled from upstairs, "Genny, come fold the rest of this laundry, please! Jeff, is that you? We have to be at the accountant's office in twenty minutes. Jonathon—answer the door when the man comes to fix the washer!"

All in one breath. Wow, I thought. If there's anyone who has to make a lot of decisions, it's her. I took to the steps again.

Mom was putting on her lipstick. She nodded toward the pile of laundry on the bed without even going out of her lip line. Jonathon was in there, too, picking up his stack.

"Mom," I said, "when you have a really tough decision to make, how do you do it?"

She froze and stared at me in the mirror. "Genevieve," she said, "are you in some kind of trouble?"

"No—not yet—but see, when I get older, I want to know how—"

"Thank heaven," she said. She closed her eyes, and I knew she was saying one of those prayers of thanks she always said when I *didn't* need stitches. "I've got to go. Look, Sweetie, when the time comes that you do have to make tough decisions, your dad and I will be right there for you. There's more in the dryer, but don't get in the repairman's way."

More decisions? In the dryer? I didn't get that one figured out until our car had pulled out of the driveway and the washing machine repairman's truck had pulled in with Jonathon down there to let him in. Solemnly I went down the steps with spiral notebook in hand. Nobody was taking me seriously. Maybe they were all too close to me to be objective.

When I got to the laundry room, the repairman was studying the back of the washer.

"I think I've found the problem, ma'am," he said.

"I'm not the ma'am," I said. "I'm the kid." And likely to stay that way, I thought, if I don't get some information soon—

He nodded, sort of sagely, I thought, and I homed in.

"Could I ask you some questions, sir?" I said.

"If it's about this brand of washer, sure."

"No, it's about making decisions. I mean, how do you do it?"

He didn't even look surprised. He put his hand in his back

pocket and pulled out a dog-eared book. "I read the manual," he said.

"Oh," I said.

"Get the stuff out of the dryer and let the man work," Jonathon said behind me. "And Rachel just called. They're coming at 6:00. She wanted to be sure Mom and Dad were going to be gone when they got here. What's up with that?"

"I don't know," I snapped. I was getting pretty cranky about this whole thing.

"Y'know, you really ought to consider switching to decaf," he said.

I ignored him.

With my hair in a new scrunchie, I was on the porch at 5:45, waiting for Marty and Rachel and studying the notebook. So far I had three things written in it.

Don't borrow trouble.

Go talk to somebody.

Read the manual.

Terrific. This little set of rules was going to see me through every crisis that lay ahead. I'd been hoping for something more like the Ten Commandments. Ah, to be a child again, blithely memorizing Bible verses, not knowing what dark evils lay just around the corner.

I was so busy peeking around the mental corner at them that I didn't see Marty's truck until he leaned on the horn and brought me right up off the wicker. Then all thoughts of the First Amendment toppled out of my head.

"Hey, Gene-veeev!" Marty yelled. He was leaning half his body out of the driver's side window.

But my eyes were on the crowd in the bed of the red pickup.

There must have been fifteen kids back there—though it was hard to tell where one set of legs ended and another one started. Somebody was totally upside down, leg sticking up against the cab with a baseball cap tottering from his toes. Everybody was screaming some variation on "Gene-veeev!"

The whole thing was so wild, Jonathon peeled open the front curtain. Rachel climbed out of the front seat and ran across the lawn to meet me. She looked like she had just taken the last Oreo without permission.

"Hi," she said. "We picked up a couple more people—"

"A *couple!*" I said. "That's our whole youth group! We could get a discount at Disneyland with that crowd."

"They're all fun."

I leaned in like a crane. I tend to do that with my neck when I'm really intense. "That isn't the point," I said. "Marty's gonna slam on the brakes or something and somebody's gonna go catapulting out of there. My luck, it'll be me."

"Marty's careful," Rachel said, voice winding up defensively.

"That'll mean a whole lot when we all get stopped by a cop," I said. "It's totally against the law."

Rachel looked over her shoulder at the squealing crowd. "I know, Gen, but if we say we won't go—we're gonna miss out. I mean, they'll have this, like, shared experience and we'll be out of it."

I looked at the crowd crammed into the back of the truck. It *would* be a bummer to sit here watching more *Matlock* reruns while they went out and did delicious stuff.

It would also be a bummer to be plastered all over the road or have to make a phone call to Dad from Juvie Hall.

I grabbed Rachel's hand. "I'm not going, Rache, and I

don't think you want to, either. If we tell them together, maybe we can actually stop the whole thing."

"So you broke up the cruisin' party, huh?" Jonathon said to me about an hour later as I was operating the microwave.

"Yeah," I said. "Rachel's gonna ask if we can all go to her house, but I have to wait until Mom and Dad get home anyway before I can go out."

He helped himself to the plate of nachos I'd just pulled out. "So what happened to your survey?"

"How did you know about that?"

"Eyes. Ears. That kind of thing."

"Huh," I said. I hadn't even known he was hanging around.

"You know, you didn't even need to take a survey," he said. "You already know how to make ethical decisions."

"I don't!"

"So what was that you did out there?"

I stopped with a Dorito in midair, still attached to the pile by a string of cheese. "I said we shouldn't go because it was stupid to—"

"Borrow trouble?"

"Well—yeah. And because it's against the law—"

"You read the manual."

"But I had to have Rachel go with me because—"

"There's always somebody you can go to."

"Yikes," I said.

Suddenly, I looked at Jonathon for probably the first time in about five years. He was twirling a piece of mozzarella around his finger, looking like Chuck E Cheese himself, and yet he did have a certain—what was it?

"Hey, Jonathon," I said slowly. "I don't have my notebook

but—how do *you* make decisions?"

He licked his fingers. "Just like you did tonight. I mean, it only figures—we were taught the same way."

"We were?"

"Sure—why else have we been going to church since the day after we were born?"

"Oh," I said.

About a thousand questions popped into my head then, and I opened my mouth to spew at least thirteen of them at the same time. But he got the here-we-go-again look on his face and put the hush-up-for-seven-seconds hand up.

"I hate to admit this," he said. "But weird as you are I think God's already got you together."

"Wow," I said—and picked up the notebook again. The Genny gene was going full tilt. "So, Jonathon," I said, "what makes you tick?"

WAKE-UP CALL

"Emily—turn out that light, please."

"OK, Mom, in a minute." I held my breath.

"*Emily!*"

She wasn't buying it. She knew that "in a minute" could mean any time before dawn.

Predictably, my bedroom door cracked open and Mom poked her head in. Her eyes were baggy with sleep.

"Do you know that it's one A.M.?" she said.

"Yeah, Mom, but I have to—"

"You have to turn out that light and get some sleep. You'll be getting up in five hours—and that isn't enough rest."

"I have to finish this paper for English."

"Is that it?" she said, nodding to the twenty-seven pages that were stacked on the bed in front of me.

I nodded.

"Heavens, Emily! How much longer can you make it?"

I sighed impatiently. "It's not how long it is—it's how *good* it is. I'm editing."

"No," she said firmly. "You're sleeping." She snapped out my overhead light and left the room.

Silently I blessed the person who invented the flashlight and clicked mine on at my paper and took refuge under my comforter.

My mom got married right out of high school and thought someday she'd go to college. But I was born, and then three years later my father died—and someday never came. She always said she was truly blessed, though, having me and her younger sister, my Aunt Joanna, as her family. She always said she didn't mind working as a clerk. She didn't want the excitement of Joanna's job as a paramedic and she'd never had the kind of dreams I had.

But for me, they weren't just dreams. It had been obvious to me since the day they told me I could skip fourth grade that God had big plans for me—and it would all mean someday I'd have a chance to make my mom's life better than it had ever been. For *me*, someday *was* going to come.

However, these days, those plans didn't seem to include sleep. It was a good thing I apparently didn't need it.

"Emily!"

Mom, all right! I thought. *Would you get a clue? I have to study. I'll sleep later.*

"Emily Oliver—are you sleeping in my class?"

My eyes twanged open, and for a chaotic moment I couldn't figure out what was so close to my eye.

Oh—it was the title of my paper, which I had rested my head on just for a minute while Mrs. Danini droned on about the quality she was expecting to see in our work.

As I jerked my head up I realized I had just drooled all over mine.

"Get to bed nights, Emily," Mrs. Danini barked. "Now, would you all double-check to be sure that your name, date, and period number are in the lower left hand corner of your cover sheet—"

I tried to shake my head clear and gingerly tested the side of my face for sleep wrinkles.

"Did you pull an all-nighter, Genius?" a voice behind me said.

I looked over my shoulder. I wasn't sure, but I thought the head of hair who sat behind me had spoken. Just to be on the safe side, I nodded at him.

"I'm with you all the way," the hair said, speaking the first words he'd uttered all year. "I started at 7:00 last night and finished at 6:00 this morning. What about you?"

"I've actually been working on it for a couple of weeks," I said.

He reached up and peeled his mop back so he could stare at me out of murky brown eyes.

"*Why?*" he said.

"Because," I said, "it's an honors class."

"I guess I hear that. I'm on probation in the honors program. I gotta make the grade on this assignment or I'm out of here." His eyes locked on me again. "But two weeks? I don't want anything that bad!"

I glanced up at Mrs. Danini who was at the front of our row waiting for the papers to be passed up. I reluctantly put mine into the hands of the girl in front of me and watched as it made its way to the front.

"Hey. Genius." Hair snapped his fingers in front of my face. "It's gone now. It's done. You can go home and sleep."

"No, I can't," I said. "I have a biology lab today. I'll be up half the night writing that up."

"Lawson?"

I nodded.

"Gotta draw every cell on the planet."

"Yeah," I said, "but I can handle it—"

"Until you fall asleep in Lawson's class. He doesn't wake you up—he gives you detention."

"Chance, I hate to interrupt that fascinating intellectual repartee you're obviously sharing with Emily," Mrs. Danini said, "but we are moving along to some Dickens. I'd like for the two of you to move with us."

"Sure," Hairy Chance said to her. To me he muttered, "See me after class. I've got something for you."

When Mrs. Danini's introduction to *A Tale of Two Cities* was finally over and the bell mercifully rang, Chance jerked his head toward the door. I followed curiously. But when he led me around the corner and plunked what looked like a bottle of aspirin into my hand, I hesitated.

"Coupla these three times a day and you can stay up the rest of your life," he said.

"But what—" I stammered.

"Don't worry about it. I got plenty—and you need 'em worse than I do."

I stared down at the plastic bottle I had curled in my fingers and then up at him. But he was already halfway down the hall.

"Aspirin?" I called after him.

"You're the genius—read the label!" was his answer.

"Stay-A-Wake," I read as Hairy Chance disappeared into the tangle of students.

I almost dropped the container and ran. Drugs? I'd been given drugs? Right here—right outside my honors class? A chorus of "Just say no!" chased through my brain as I stared at it again.

"Johnson & Johnson," the fine print said. Didn't they make baby powder?

It wasn't a prescription, and it wasn't in one of those little plastic bags they'd been warning us about since third grade. There was even a price still stuck to the top. $2.99. I was pretty sure illegal drugs had to cost more than that.

At lunch I read every microscopic word on the label. *Non-habit forming. Safe if used as directed. Stay up the rest of your life.*

Actually, the label didn't include that last one, but Hairy Chance's words kept curling around in my head, all through history, all through biology—especially when I pulled my eyes away from the microscope and rested my chin in my hand, just for a minute—and Mr. Lawson said, "Your eyes are at half-mast, Emily. I give detentions for sleeping in class."

Hairy Chance had been right about that.

I raised my hand. "Mr. Lawson," I said, "may I go get a drink of water?"

As I hurried down the hall, I made sure the container of pills was still in my pocket.

Hairy Chance was right about *everything*, I decided later. I stayed awake through biology—*and* the after-school Student Council meeting—*and* the youth group meeting that night at church—*and* the four hours of homework I put in after that. Even after I finished drawing "every cell on the planet"—Hairy had been right about that, too—I lay awake in the dark with my heart racing happily.

"I'm going to live the life you have planned for me, God," I whispered as I did every night.

Only that night I didn't immediately lapse into a coma the

way I usually did. I didn't go to sleep until almost two. I was pretty thankful for those safe-if-used-as-directed pills the next morning.

I didn't have another conversation with Hairy Chance for a week. There was no opportunity with our noses pasted into *A Tale of Two Cities* every day. But at last Mrs. Danini put us into discussion groups, and Hairy ended up in mine.

"All *righty* then!" I sang out as I whipped a sheet of paper from my binder and twiddled my pen. "Why was it the best of times?"

Hairy flipped his mane back to look at me. "You're hyper these days," he said.

"Thanks to you," I said.

"To *me?*" His murky brown eyes looked puzzled for a minute before he said, "Oh. You mean—?"

"Yep." I tapped my pen four times on my desk top.

"You should chill out, dude," Hairy said. "Too much of a good thing'll kill you."

I kept tapping my pen, but my mind flipped immediately away from the best and worst of times to Hairy's words of advice—the ones that had spurred my dreams on this week. He'd never said anything about too much of a good thing before.

Nor had he ever told me how to get to sleep after I was finished being awake. That day was Friday, and usually I crashed early on Fridays so I could get caught up. That evening my body refused to take a dive. I hadn't even taken my two pills at dinner time—the first dose I'd missed in a week—but even after Mom had left for a weekend church retreat and Joanna and I had polished off a pepperoni pizza, I was still pacing like a caged tiger.

Joanna watched me with her bright brown eyes.

"Girl, you are like a cat in a room full of rocking chairs," she said. "Sit down, would you?"

I did, but I bounced up about seven seconds later.

"What are you doing?" she said.

"I'm going to make us some popcorn," I said.

I could feel her eyes boring into my back as I dug in the cabinet for some Orville Redenbacher.

"You know what you remind me of?" she said.

"What?" Ah, there was the box.

"That hamster you used to have. What was its name?"

"Jethro," I said. A pang went through me and I set the box down hard on the counter.

"Jethro, yeah. He used to tear around on that hamster wheel like he was running from the FBI. That's what you look like flitting around here." Her voice broke off. "Emily? Emily, Honey, what's the matter?"

I was leaning over the counter sobbing.

"Jethro died," I blubbered.

"But that was six years ago!"

"It was awful, Joanna," I sobbed. I was crying so hard I could hardly choke out the words.

Suddenly Joanna held me out at arm's length and pried one of my weepy eyes open with practiced fingers. Another set of fingers went to my wrist as she studied the clock over my head. I knew she wasn't Aunt Joanna now. She was Paramedic Hoffman.

"Emily, your pulse is racing like a jack rabbit's. Your pupils—" The sharp brown eyes went through me. "Emily—have you taken something?"

"Nothing illegal!" I said.

"But something?"

I nodded.

"What? What did you take? Show me!"

I reached into my pocket and produced the bottle. As she read the label, her lip curled.

"How long have you been taking these?" she said.

"A week. But it says they're safe if you take them as directed, and I—I didn't take any more than it said."

Her eyebrows shot up. "You've taken six of these a day for a week?"

I nodded—and blubbered—and shook.

She unscrewed the cap and dumped the pills into the sink. The garbage disposal gobbled them up.

"What are you doing?" I cried. "I need those!"

"For what? What could you possibly need this trash for?"

"To stay awake! I have to study! I have to have a 4.0. I have to get scholarships—and it all starts now—it's God's plan!"

"*What?*" Aunt Joanna's face twisted. "It's God's plan that you ruin your *health?*"

"No! But I want to be somebody! I want to take care of Mom!" I shook my head until it started spinning, and I had to clutch at the counter to stay up. Aunt Joanna grabbed my arm and led me to the couch where she sat beside me and held me—hard.

"What is this plan of God's that you're talking about?" she said.

"I'm supposed to *succeed*—I'm supposed to use my brain for something. God wouldn't have made me smart if that weren't his plan—"

"*His* plan—not yours!"

"But I have to work hard to do my part!"

"Your part isn't to work a miracle, Emily. The miracles are God's department. You can only do what is humanly possible, Honey. Doing stuff like this to yourself just shows me you have no faith that God can make it happen. Don't you see that?"

"But Mom—"

"It's lovely that you want to make your mother's life better, but Emily, that's God's job, too. If he wants you to do that, he'll provide a way. And it isn't through drugs—over-the-counter or otherwise."

The sobs were starting to slow down, but it was still hard for me to make sense out of any of it.

"I don't know why I'm crying!" I said. "I didn't even like Jethro that much. He pooped all over my room."

"When did you take the last pill?" Joanna said.

"Lunch."

"You're coming down from a major caffeine high. Any little thing could set you off." Her eyes were paramedic serious. "This stuff is not in itself habit-forming—but the habit of relying on something besides God to get you through—that's habit-forming. Who got you started on these anyway?"

"Hairy Chance," I said.

"Don't listen to any more of his advice. And don't try to do God's job for him. God's bigger than—Hairy. He's bigger than everything."

The tears swelled up in my throat again. "What about Jethro?" I said.

She chuckled softly. "I think some warm milk will take care of Jethro."

By Monday, most of the Stay-A-Wake was out of my system and my insides had stopped going a bazillion miles an hour. In Honors English, I didn't tap my pen on the desk even once while we were taking the *Two Cities* quiz. I was wide awake— from eight hours' sleep.

When we were handing in the quizzes, Hairy poked me in the back.

"What did you do, Genius, take some downers?"

I turned around and curled my lip at him. "No," I said, "I don't need that stuff."

"You coulda fooled me last week."

"No," I said, "*you* fooled *me*."

But then I turned around, because there was really no point in arguing with that mop of hair. He'd been wrong—about *everything*.

A MOVING STORY

When Hank came home that day, the hot dogs were burning and the kids were plugged into *Batman* or *Power Rangers* or something. It could have been *Days of Our Lives* for all I knew. I was staring out the kitchen window while the turkey franks turned to charcoal in the skillet.

But Hank didn't yell. He never yells. He just turned off the burner and said, "Kate, I come home expecting 'The Three Billy Goats Gruff' and I get 'The Three Little Pigs Do Backdraft.'"

"Oh no!" My voice spiraled up in despair. I started to rush toward the stove, but he caught me gently by the arm and looked at me with those little blue eyes through his John Lennon glasses.

"Where are the kids?" he said. "Have you cooked them, too?"

"They're in the family room watching—whatever."

Hank's eyebrows went up, which was easy to understand. Usually when he got home from work, Saralinda, age seven-going-on-thirteen, was playing the role of Cinderella, Snow White, or, in her latest appearance, the troll, and Toby, age six-and-holding, was portraying everything else with the versatility of Dustin Hoffman—all under my expert direction *while* I was concocting turkey stir-fry or chicken paprikash. No wonder Hank was looking askance at this bad scene from a teen horror film.

"I'll go turn off the TV," I said.

But Hank kept his hold on my arm. "One afternoon in a comatose state isn't going to fry their brains," he said. "You're obviously in worse shape than they are. Sit down."

I plopped down miserably at the table in the breakfast nook, and Hank brought over two little bottles of apple juice and joined me.

"All right, Kate, spill it," he said. "Your guts—not the juice."

Then he grinned, which he managed to do a lot, in spite of the sadness lines etched around his eyes. Allison, his wife, had died nine months before. He could still smile, though, and tease me by calling me Kate when everyone else called me Kathryn. He could also still say all the right things when I was there taking care of his kids after school every day.

But I was pretty sure he wasn't going to be able to do it this time.

"So what's with the long face?" he said.

"I guess my parents haven't told you we're moving," I said.

He blinked at me, and then smiled a half-smile. "You live across the street from people for ten years, you think you know them. But they get ready to move to a ritzier neighborhood and suddenly you're chopped liver."

"No!" I wailed. "We're not moving to a ritzier neighborhood, we're moving to another state!"

"Which one?"

"Colorado!"

Hank gave a low whistle. "That's a long way from Connecticut."

"No kidding—a long way from all my friends and my school and my church and everything I've ever known." My eyes were filling up for the twentieth time that day. "This is my junior year. How can they do this to me?"

I put my face in my hands so I could maintain some semblance of dignity while I blubbered. Hank tactfully switched to his I'm-going-to-pretend-I-don't-see-you-getting-snot-all-over-the-tablecloth voice.

"Did your dad lose his job?"

"No, he got a better one. More money and all that stuff that's so important to—them."

"'Them' being your parents?"

"Yes, and please don't say what every adult I talked to at church said to me yesterday. 'You'll make new friends so fast.' 'Don't you want your dad to be happy?' 'You're only sixteen—it's not the end of the world.'" I grabbed two fists full of my hair to keep from exploding. "Well, it's the end of *my* world! Where am I going to find friends like mine that like to do the stuff I like to do? We see foreign films and talk about them over fondue and sit around and compare how we see God in our lives. Are there actually going to be people in Colorado who won't look at me like I'm an alien because of the way I dress? Is there going to be anybody there who accepts that I laugh like a chicken?"

Hank shook his head. "I don't know—although I don't think there will be anybody there who understands the way you dress. I always thought you looked like an unmade bed." He squeezed my hand. "I'll miss you. Nobody can match your spaghetti sauce."

I started to cry again. "You're the first person who hasn't tried to make me feel better," I said.

"I can't. This has got to be hard for you."

"You could say that." I put a stranglehold on the apple juice bottle. "My parents are being totally inconsiderate. I mean, what if there are no schools there that have an Advanced Placement program or a decent art teacher—all the stuff I need for my future? And what about you—what are you supposed to do for a baby sitter now? They haven't thought of anybody but my dad."

The sympathetic softness in Hank's eyes faded.

"I can't listen," he said.

"To what?" I said.

"Parent bashing. If you think your dad is being 'inconsiderate,' you need to tell him, not me. Here."

I took the Kleenex box he passed me and blew my nose noisily. "What good would that do?" I said. "It isn't going to change their minds."

"Neither is telling me," Hank said. "Look, I can burn hot dogs just as well as you can. You go home and talk to your dad."

My father, I thought as I marched across the street and into our foyer, was the last person I even wanted to *see* right now. Ever since Saturday night when he and my mother had told me over a platter of chicken nachos at Chili's that at semester break we were moving two thousand miles away, I'd been seething. Moving was the one thing my dad *hadn't* done to me. He'd worked out of town, leaving me fatherless for weeks at a time. He'd changed jobs four times, causing me any number of sleepless nights worrying about whether there would be enough money. Taking me away from the friends I'd had since preschool—when chances are this wouldn't last either—was about more than I could take. When he'd told me, I'd had this horrible urge to pour salsa on his head.

And I'm not like that. I try to live by the example of Christ. Plus I make way-above-decent grades and never give my parents any grief. Yeah, I'm a little bizarre when it comes to things like getting up at four in the morning to watch the sun rise. But I didn't deserve to be punished like this. It was enough to make me hurl things, and in spite of Hank's advice, I wanted to avoid my father lest I hurl something at *him*.

But he was standing right at the top of the stairs when I got there. The stairs that for my whole life I had crept down on Christmas Eves and sat on in my pajamas to listen to adult parties late at night. I started to cry again.

"What's wrong, Honey?" Dad said. "Kathryn?"

I bit back, *What do you think is wrong?* and just looked at him.

"Is it this moving thing?" he said.

I couldn't help it. I rolled my eyes. He hates it when I roll my eyes.

"Sit," he said. He pulled me down to the top step by my elbow and sat by me. My dad is no small man. You don't argue with him.

"Let's go," he said.

"What?"

"Tell me what's going on in your head. You're so mad you could spit nails. Let's hear it."

"What good would it do?" I said. It did feel like I was spitting nails. "I don't mean to be disrespectful, Dad, but you're going to do exactly what you want anyway."

"Where is this coming from?" he said.

Normally at this point I would have taken a temperature reading on his voice before I plunged in, but this wasn't "normally."

"You never stay in one job!" I said. "And so far I've dealt with that, but this is so unfair. Now I have to leave my whole life behind while you—"

There was a pause.

"While I what?" he said.

"I don't even know! Can't you find a job *here* you can be happy with?"

He pulled at his mustache before he answered. "Sure," he said. "But I know I'm not going to be unhappy with the job in Colorado or I wouldn't be moving you like this. Don't you think I know how you must feel?"

"No."

"I think I do, because you and I are so much alike. The reason it's been so hard for me to find the right job is that, like you, I see things differently from other people. I have to be able to apply my creativity and the things that make me unique or I just don't feel like I belong. Finally someone has seen that and offered me a place where I can do that. That's a gift from God I can't toss away."

I looked down at my hands while tears drained silently down my face. I hated to admit it, but it made sense.

"I get it," I mumbled.

He put his big bear arms around me and held me.

You'd think that would have been the end of it. After all, I wasn't mad at my dad anymore. I understood why we were going. I could start packing and planning a going-away party for myself.

But that wasn't the end of it. There was this pain in my chest that kept me awake. And these tears that splashed down on my history book when I tried to study. And these waves of fear that came over me every time anybody said something "cheerful" like, "Colorado? Cool! The skiing is so much better there!"

After a week of that, my question was, "God, where are you? I'm being this wonderful, understanding daughter—why am I still so miserable?"

So miserable that I didn't have the energy for full-scale productions of "Beauty and the Beast" over at Hank's.

"Then let's go to the park," Saralinda whined at me. "I'm sick of TV."

At least there I could just sit and envy their carefree existence while they cavorted on the play equipment. That's what I was doing when Toby swung by his knees on the jungle gym so hard that he banged his head on the next set of bars. The blood was spurting out of his forehead before he hit the ground.

I know it didn't take ten minutes to get him into the car and to the emergency room, and I'm sure it wasn't another five before Hank rushed in, his face the color of Cream of Wheat. But it seemed like hours before it was all over and Hank came out to the waiting room with a big grin on his weary face.

"He's going to be fine," he said as he slumped down next to me.

I lunged over and hugged him, sandwiching a sleeping Saralinda between us. When I pulled back, he was still smiling, but the sadness lines were carved deeply into his face.

"How do you stand it when this bad stuff happens to you?" I said.

Hank ran his hand over Saralinda's hair. "They say God doesn't give each of us more than we can handle." He twitched an eyebrow. "But sometimes I feel like he has me mixed up with somebody else, and I get all their stuff, too."

I could feel my tears coming back, and I put my hand over the pain in my chest.

Hank leaned back and put his arm across the back of my chair. "All I know is what I had to learn when Allison died. God doesn't guarantee that just because you're a Christian you won't be knocked down or even that when bad things happen you'll suffer less than non-Christians."

I gave him a dark look.

"I know," he said. "I asked him what good he was, then, several times during my really black time. But here's what he led me to, Kate. He does help you *through* your loss or your fear or whatever so you can find his healing love *in* your pain. Long after you've gone through it and have come out stronger, your nonbelieving friends are still struggling."

One of my tears dropped down on Saralinda's chubby face. "I feel stupid," I said.

"Why?"

"Because here I am whining about having to move away, and you've lost your wife and you almost lost your son—"

"And I'm about to lose the world's best baby sitter. But, Kathryn, your problems are your problems. They have to be worked *through*—and that's what you're doing. This is a big change in your life. God can help you, but he isn't going to spare you the hurt that's involved."

I laughed through a glob of tears. "Nice guy."

"Kind—compassionate—but I'd never describe God as 'nice.'" He squeezed my shoulder. "If you let God help you through this, you're going to have the assurance that he'll always be there for whatever else is coming your way."

"There's going to be more, isn't there?" I said, scowling.

"Yeah, sometimes life's kind of like a train—coming at you. But you can't think about that. You just deal with now."

"So it's OK that I don't feel happy about this move yet?"

"Perfectly normal and not even a little bit unchristian." He looked down at Saralinda. "They're going to keep Toby overnight. Let's get the Princess home and maybe you can whip up some of that spaghetti sauce of yours and we'll invite your parents over." He twinkled his little blue eyes at me through the John Lennon glasses. "We can all cry in it, huh?"

"No problem there," I said. "There're plenty more tears where these came from."

JULIANNA'S LATEST ALBUM

It wasn't up there.

It wasn't up there.

At first Julianna thought she'd missed it and scanned the list, poised to squeal the instant her eyes caught on her name.

But it wasn't up there.

She hadn't made Ensemble.

"Way to go, Joe!" a female voice said. That redheaded alto.

"Sara! We're awesome!" the boy said back. The tall tenor.

Their hand slapping was happening at the edge of a nightmare, because it wasn't up there. She hadn't made Ensemble. And she'd *known* she would.

"Rehearsals at 7:00 A.M.?" Sara said.

"If you can't handle it, there're ten other altos waitin' to take your place," Joe said. "Hey—you want this girl's place?"

For the first time Julianna pried her eyes away from the list. Joe's eyebrows were cocked expectantly. "Sara obviously doesn't want the honor. So take her place, would you?"

Sara nudged him sharply.

"What?" he said, as she dragged him away. "What did I say?"

"She tried out for Ensemble, tofu-for-brains," Sara hissed to him. "Don't you remember?"

Julianna tossed back her mane of blonde, just in case they should look back. Nobody needed to know that her throat was clogged with a thousand waiting tears.

The bell rang. She pulled her notebook to her chest and moved slowly toward the chorus room—the last place she wanted to go now.

The room was a cacophony of congratulatory squeals and hugs. Julianna wriggled through it, head down, and slumped into the alto section. A couple of the waiting tears got clearance for takeoff, and she smacked at them fiercely.

"All right, folks," Mrs. Christopher sang out. She always sounded like she was singing. Right now it was a funeral dirge.

"I trust you all looked at the list—"

"No! Am I on it?" Joe said.

"Congratulations to our new Ensemble. You realize—yeah?—that in a school that prides itself on its arts programs, those people are the very best we have—"

Then my name should be up there! Julianna hissed to herself. *I AM the best. Why else would my parents have gotten a variance to send me here? Why else would everyone have been telling me since I was seven years old that they'd be seeing me on the cover of my own album someday?*

"—naturally I could only select fourteen, but the rest of you who auditioned, don't be discouraged. You will have other chances."

"I'm trying out again next year," said the girl next to Julianna. "A sophomore almost never makes Ensemble."

Julianna looked at her in surprise. That girl—what was her name?—Betsy?—had belted out "Memory" from *Cats* like Bette Midler. She was only a sophomore—like Julianna?

"And folks—" Mrs. Christopher peered at them over her music stand— "No back-stabbing, yeah? If you have a problem with my selections, come and speak to me personally."

School was out at 2:05. At 2:07 Julianna was tapping on the chorus office door.

"My 'new kid'!" Mrs. Christopher sang. "I've been waiting for a chance to get to know you a little better." She pulled two stacks of music from a chair. "These first few weeks of school are such a zoo with all these auditions—please sit down—but now we can get on with the business of singing, yeah?"

Julianna nodded.

"So—what can I do for you?"

Julianna open her mouth—and then slammed it shut. She'd planned to tell Mrs. Christopher that she obviously had chosen her "pets" for the Ensemble, and that Julianna and people like Betsy-what's-her-name ought to be on the list.

But this was the first time she'd really noticed anything about Mrs. Christopher except that she had too much salt-and-pepper hair for her tiny face. Now dazzling kind blue eyes sparkled at her. She smiled a smile that said, "I have all the time in the world for you."

Julianna cleared her throat. "I wanted to talk to you—about—why I didn't make Ensemble."

"Why do you think you should have?" Mrs. Christopher said.

Julianna's eyes leapt up. "Well—OK—I've been singing since I was way little. You couldn't be in the junior choir at church unless you could read, so I learned in about three months—just so I could sing—that's how much it means to me."

More than a few of the clogged-up tears were making their escape. Silently Mrs. Christopher pushed a box of Kleenex toward her.

"Like—from the very beginning, they always gave me all the solos—and people tell me *every Sunday* what a gift I have—I mean, that's why I changed schools. I didn't even take Honors English because it's the same period as chorus."

"What do you plan to do with your singing, Julianna?" Mrs. Christopher said.

"The Lord meant for me to be a singer. That's what I want to do with my life." Julianna snorted through the gunk that came with the tears. "I practically have my first album cover designed."

"Not making Ensemble was a real blow, then?"

Julianna could only nod.

Mrs. Christopher sat on the edge of her desk and touched Julianna's hand lightly. "Julianna, I don't pull punches with my students. You have a sweet voice, and you know your stuff. I'm delighted to have you. But, my dear, I don't think you're going to be a professional singer. Maybe your voice will mature—I've been wrong—but right *now* you aren't Ensemble material."

Julianna stared as Mrs. Christopher's face blurred into the tears.

"I'm going to go now, OK?" she said.

And before Mrs. Christopher could answer, she'd slammed two doors behind her.

There was no question about what to do now. She didn't even discuss it with her parents. They'd probably have a stroke when they found out she was dropping chorus altogether to sign up for Honors English—when they'd gone to all the trouble to have her transferred.

But third period she put the pink schedule change form on

Mrs. Christopher's desk. The blue eyes met hers sharply.

"I've already missed two weeks of Honors," Julianna said woodenly.

Mrs. Christopher stood up. "I won't sign this unless you'll do something for me."

For you? Julianna snapped to herself. *The same person who took my dreams and wadded them up like a rough draft?*

"You know about our Career Exploration Program here, yeah?" Mrs. Christopher was saying. "You can spend one day with a professional and get a feel for her career. If you will spend a career exploration day with me, I'll sign your schedule change."

"But—what career?"

Mrs. Christopher threw her bushy head back and hooted. "I often ask myself that!" she said. "I'm a music professional, my dear. And I want you to see what that can mean."

At 7:00 the next morning, Julianna was in the rehearsal hall, gritting her teeth as the Ensemble practiced. At 2:00 that afternoon, she was in the empty chorus room, counting. She'd heard almost two hundred kids sing in one day. And in the midst of it, she'd seen Mrs. Christopher make a kid laugh when his recently changed voice did a two-octave lurch. She'd seen her spend ten minutes in her office calming a crying girl and the next twenty discussing cruelty versus manners with the class. She'd seen her teach music theory to kids who looked like potential dropouts and play piano for a struggling soloist with one hand while eating a sandwich with the other. Her hair got wilder and her smile got wider, and at the end of the day she kicked her shoes playfully across the room.

Still—Julianna didn't see what any of it had to do with her. "I'm through now?" she said.

"Not in the slightest! You're coming home with me. I called your mom—she was glad to get rid of that long face for an evening! Get your sweater. The day is still young."

Julianna was less than enthusiastic as they pulled up to an almost-all-glass house with a grand piano displayed in one huge pane. But once inside, when Mrs. Christopher said, "Play it if you want. I'll start dinner," it was hard to keep scowling.

The piano quivered at the slightest touch. So did the violin lying on top of it. The living room was checkered with piles of music, and one huge cabinet bulged with tapes and CDs.

"Who are you?" a tall kid with a backpack full of textbooks asked her as he passed through.

"Nice to see ya—want a Coke?—is she the slave driver at school that she is at home?" That's what the other three said as they passed through. All four of Mrs. Christopher's almost-grown kids tinkered with the piano and flipped the remote on the CD player. At the dinner table they argued happily about the "Should Amy Grant have crossed over into secular music?" question. And after supper they all sang barbershop quartet in the kitchen while they did the dishes. Julianna sang alto.

"Aren't any of you ever going to get your own places?" Mrs. Christopher asked them, laughing. "When you have kids, Julianna, make them sign a contract at birth that they'll move out when they're eighteen."

Julianna felt strangely content for a minute. It looked like a happy life, with music and love at work and at home. But she shook her head at herself. It wasn't an album cover.

At 7:00, Mrs. Christopher tossed Julianna her sweater.

"We'll be at The Dream Machine," she sang out to her family, and ushered Julianna to the car.

"What's The Dream Machine?" Julianna asked.

"It's an alternative to album covers," Mrs. Christopher said.

Actually it looked like a cafe. Inside were small tables clustered in front of a stage lit up like a Las Vegas casino, and Julianna barely had a Coke in front of her before an MC with dimples came out, turned everybody inside out with his jokes, and introduced Elizabeth Louise Somebody, who sang. And then Blair Somebody, who danced. And then even Chuckles Somebody who juggled five Rubik's Cubes.

They were all good, Julianna thought, yet none of them was Michael W. Smith. But that didn't seem to matter to anybody, including the audience. Because eventually, everyone *in* the audience got up there, beaming under the lights, and did his or her thing. Even Mrs. Christopher.

Julianna had never heard her sing before, beyond belting out the alto part when the section was clueless. Microphone in hand, she eased out "Unforgettable" and made Natalie Cole sound like a frog, as far as Julianna was concerned. She knew she'd hear it in her memory-ear a thousand times—Mrs. Christopher's voice all velvet and soft and deep and rich. Julianna wrapped herself in it.

And then it hit her. Mrs. Christopher was wonderful—but she wasn't good enough to make it cutting albums. She must have had that dream at one time. Everyone in the room must have thought that when they were fifteen.

But they were still singing—and tap dancing—and juggling Rubik's Cubes. And they were happy. They must have figured out God's real plan for them in there somewhere.

On the way home, she and Mrs. Christopher sang together. "Rebecca St. James, eat your heart out," Mrs. Christopher laughed softly when they pulled up to Julianna's front door. "There's something to be said for doing it for the joy of it."

Julianna reached into her purse and pulled out the pink slip. "I need to leave this with you," she said. And she wadded it up into a lump.

"Here's where *that* belongs," Mrs. Christopher said, dropping it into the litter bag. Then she looked hard at Julianna. "I'm not trying to push you into teaching," she said. "I just wanted you to see that you can still be a professional, still have music in your life, without being a star."

"Thanks," Julianna said huskily. The tears were circling the airport again.

She *was* grateful, she thought as she buried her head in the pillow later. Tomorrow it was all going to have a new perspective. But tonight there had to be a good cry.

After all, it would have been such a *hot* album cover.

DREAMS

"What happened, Liz?" Vicki said as she passed me in the hall behind the examining rooms.

I smoothed a Band-Aid over my arm and winced. "Another scratch," I said. "My fourth one this week."

"You have to watch those killer cats," she said. "Although if I stopped to do first aid every time a patient got me I'd be standing here at the medicine cabinet half the day."

It was her way of saying, "So stop being a wimp and get back to work," and I was about to, when she popped her head back around the corner and added, "Oh, there's a phone call for you. Line two. And then get the Callahans and Muffin into D."

Hooray, I said to myself. *I love Muffin and the Callahans. Last time they brought that mutt in here I had to wrestle her to the floor just so Dr. Knowles could listen to her heartbeat. I doubt that dog has a heart.*

I was still mumbling when I picked up the phone and punched line two.

"What?" Chad said on the other end.

"What?" I shouted back from mine. It was practically impossible to have a conversation with fifteen dogs yapping twenty feet away. "Talk fast—I have to get back to work."

"There's an opening down here," Chad said.

I could feel my eyebrows springing up. "At the theater?"

185

"Yeah—one of the stagehands has to quit and they need somebody starting next week. The pay's lousy—"

But it doesn't matter, I finished for him. Any of us Drama Club maniacs would have paid *them* to let us work at the summer stock theater.

"I told them about your tech work at Webster High," Chad said, "and they were impressed." He snorted into the phone. "I told them you were almost as good as I am."

Behind me, Vicki was tapping her pencil on the counter—and beyond her in the waiting room, Muffin was chewing up a magazine while the Callahans looked on.

"What do I do?" I hissed at Chad.

"Call this number—by Saturday."

I scratched the number on the back of a heartworms pamphlet and stuffed it into my jeans pocket.

"Muffin. Room D," Vicki said curtly.

I barely heard her. There might actually be a way to get out of this zoo. That was all I could think about as I took on Muffin and the Callahans.

"It's the perfect opportunity for you," my dad had said the day he told me he'd gotten me a job at the Moody Valley Veterinary Hospital. "You've always wanted to be a vet, so this will give you a chance to work in the business for the summer. Get your feet wet."

He hadn't been kidding about that last part. I'd been peed on by everything from a German shepherd to an iguana—and none of it was reinforcing my dream of being a veterinarian.

The truth was—I hadn't had that dream since I was about twelve, and certainly not since I'd gotten involved in the theater at school. I'd never gotten a high from looking down some cocker spaniel's throat the way I did running a light board and painting scenery.

But Dad had watched me ride our horses and groom them and feed them since I was six, and—bingo—I was shoveling pills into house cats who would cheerfully shred me to ribbons if given the chance. Grooming my own horses was one thing. Playing Keep-Away with Doberman pinschers all day was another.

Dad was leaning against the fence on the west corral when I got home that night, observing Lolly, our chestnut mare.

"Look at this gal, Lizzie," he said. "She's absolutely square."

"You think she'll foal this weekend?" I said.

"Oh yeah. I'll be waking you up. They always deliver in the middle of the night."

I hiked up onto the fence and looked at poor miserable Lolly. I'd helped bring her first colt into the world. It had been cool, I had to admit. But did I want to do that—for the rest of my life?

"Chad called me today," I said. "He says they have an opening at the summer stock theater for a stagehand—"

"He's a fool to take a job like that," Dad said. He took a sip of his iced tea and squinted into the fading sun. "They don't pay half of what you're making and it won't prepare him for his future. What does he want to do when he's out of school?"

"Dad, he already works—"

"I'm proud of you, Sugar," he said, and he reached over and squeezed my shoulder. "You've got your head on straight. You know what you want and you're going after it. The money you're making with Knowles is really going to help out with college. Your mother and I can pay tuition, we've told you that, but the rest needs to come from you."

I stared at him. He had the whole conversation started, discussed, and over before he even knew what it was about.

"You have a God-given gift for working with animals," he said. "I'm glad to see you using it."

"Feeding people's house pets isn't exactly using it, Dad," I said. "I haven't touched a horse since I've been there, and besides, I don't—"

"I'll talk to Knowles," he said, and then tossed the remains of his iced tea on the ground. "Come on, let's get these horses fed."

My father and Dr. Knowles go way back to veterinary school. Dad never finished because his father died and he had to keep the family's feed store on its feet until he could sell it. Somehow he never did.

He and Dr. Knowles were still good friends, which is probably why when I got to work the next morning, Vicki scowled at me and said, "You're going out on a ranch call with the doctor today."

"Me?" I said.

"No, Madonna," she snapped back. Vicki had been working there three years and had probably never left the office.

"Do *you* want to do it?" I said.

"It doesn't matter what I want. He specifically asked for you."

Somehow that didn't thrill me. Every attempt to expose me to the wonders of veterinary medicine was making me feel guiltier and guiltier about wanting to get the Sam Hill out of there and into a theater.

"He colicked," Mr. Crowley told us, stroking his mahogany-colored gelding's mane.

Dr. Knowles ran a hand down Sultan's forelock. "Get some sand in your belly, old buddy?"

"He wants to roll," said Crowley. He looked at me. "That could be fatal."

I knew that. A horse would roll on the ground and try to eliminate the severe pain in his stomach and end up twisting his insides irreversibly and dying.

"You want me to walk him?" I said to Dr. Knowles.

He nodded. "Listen for bowel sounds. I'll mix up some bran and Metamucil."

Fabulous. I could be up in the first beam right now, focusing a state-of-the-art lighting instrument—and here I was listening for bowel sounds.

But I'd done it enough times with our seven horses to know I was possibly saving the animal's life, and that was nice. Besides, I had everybody giving me all these chances in a field where a lot of people, like Vicki, didn't get past the phone and thermometers. I had my parents willing to pay for most of my education and enough money in this job to handle the rest myself.

"I really ought to stop wishing for some out-of-reach dream and just go for this vet thing," I said to Sultan. He rewarded me with a major bowel gurgle.

"Fabulous," I told him.

It couldn't have been much after 4:00 A.M. when my dad woke me up the next morning. Lolly was about to deliver.

By the time I got to the barn, the feet had already poked their way into the world, and within twenty minutes the rest of a gooey little filly was lying in the hay next to her mother.

"Well, look here, Lolly," Dad crooned. "You got you a beautiful little girl."

Actually, I thought the foal was pretty homely with the birth sac stuck to her like wet cobwebs and her hair standing up in punky spikes, but Dad kept saying, "Hello, pretty lady," as he broke the sac and pushed the mucus away from her nostrils.

"Now the fun starts," he said to me as Lolly proceeded to bathe her new baby with her tongue. "Hopefully she'll be standing up and nursing within two hours so she gets those good antibodies into her from Mama."

I knew all that, but I watched my father with rapt attention. His face was actually glowing, and his eyes were shining with the work he was doing. I was going through the motions as I'd done so many times before, waiting for the cord to separate so I could bathe the foal's navel with iodine—all those things.

But for my father, this was a miracle and he was taking part in it with a kind of reverence. To him, it was God's work. For me, it was just a job.

That's when it occurred to me that working at the animal hospital, preparing for my career as a veterinarian, was the spinning out of *his* dream, not mine. If I didn't feel the joy of it, I was cheating him as much as I was myself.

I shoved my hands in my jeans pockets as I watched him, and my fingers curled around the heartworms pamphlet. It was

Saturday, and the phone number for the theater was right there at my fingertips.

"There she goes!" Dad cried.

Lolly's foal was gathering her legs under her. With one courageous heave she went up on her feet—and fell flat on her homely little nose.

I may fall on my face, too, I thought, *but I need to at least try to sort this out.*

"Dad," I said. "You believe in dreams, don't you?"

My father didn't even blink. "You bet I do," he said nodding at Lolly's baby. "Here's one come true, right here."

I sighed a huge breath and plopped myself down in the hay. "Then, Dad," I said, "—can we talk?"

FOCUS ON THE FAMILY

———— Like This Book? ————

Then you'll love *Brio* magazine! Written especially for teen girls, it's packed each month with 32 pages on everything from fiction and faith to fashion, food . . . even guys! Best of all, it's all from a Christian perspective! But don't take our word for it. Instead, see for yourself by requesting a complimentary copy.

Simply write: Focus on the Family, Colorado Springs, CO 80995. In Canada, write: P.O. Box 9800, Stn. Terminal, Vancouver, BC V6B 4G3. Mention that you saw this offer in the back of this book. You may also call 1-800-232-6459 (in Canada, call 1-800-661-9800).

Focus on the Family is an organization that is dedicated to helping you and your family establish lasting, loving relationships with each other and the Lord. It's why we exist! If we can assist you or your family in any way, please feel free to contact us. We'd love to hear from you!

You may also visit our Web site (www.family.org) to learn more about the ministry or find out if there is a Focus on the Family office in your country.

9DMXNR